Study Guide
for

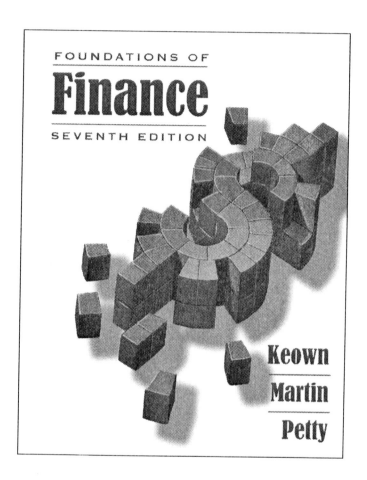

FOUNDATIONS OF
Finance
SEVENTH EDITION

Keown

Martin

Petty

Arthur J. Keown
Virginia Polytechnic Institute and State University

John D. Martin
Baylor University

J. William Petty
Baylor University

Pearson Prentice Hall

Boston San Francisco New York
London Toronto Sydney Tokyo Singapore Madrid
Mexico City Munich Paris Cape Town Hong Kong Montreal

Acquisitions Editor: Tessa O'Brien
Editorial Project Manager: Kerri McQueen
Production Editor: Alison Eusden
Manufacturing Buyer: Linda Cox

Pearson Prentice Hall™ is a trademark of Pearson Education, Inc.

Prentice Hall
is an imprint of

www.pearsonhighered.com

2 3 4 5 V036 13 12 11 10
ISBN-13: 978-0-13-611366-9
ISBN-10: 0-13-611366-4

CONTENTS

CHAPTER 1

An Introduction to the Foundations of Financial Management

Orientation: This chapter lays a foundation for what will follow. First, it focuses on the goal of the firm, followed by a review of the legal forms of business organization, and a discussion of the tax implications relating to financial decisions. Ten Principles that form the foundations of financial management then follow.

I.   Goal of the Firm

    A.   In this book, maximization of shareholder wealth, by which we mean maximization of the total market value of the firm's common stock, will be designated as the firm's goal. To understand this goal and its inclusive nature, it is first necessary to understand the difficulties involved with the frequently suggested goal of profit maximization.

    B.   We have chosen the goal of shareholder wealth maximization because the effects of all financial decisions are included in this goal.

    C.   In order to employ this goal, we need not consider every price change to be a market interpretation of the worth of our decisions. What we do focus on is the effect that our decision *should* have on the stock price if everything were held constant.

II.   Five Principles that Form the Foundations of Finance

    A.   **Principle 1: Cash Flow Is What Matters.** In measuring value we will use cash flows rather than accounting profits because it is only cash flows that the firm receives and is able to reinvest. In addition, in making business decisions, we will concern ourselves with only what happens as a result of that decision.

B. **Principle 2: Money Has a Time Value.** Almost all financial decisions involve comparing money in different time periods, perhaps investing today and receiving returns later, or borrowing money today and paying it off later. A dollar received today is worth more than a dollar received in the future because of the time value of money.

C. **Principle 3: Risk Requires a Reward.** There is a risk-return trade-off in finance: We won't take additional risk unless we expect to be compensated with additional return. Almost all financial decisions involve some sort of risk-return trade-off.

D. **Principle 4: Market Prices Are Generally Right.** In general, the markets are quick to impound new information into stock prices and the prices tend to be correct.

E. **Principle 5: Conflicts of Interest Cause Agency Problems.** As a result of the agency problem, managers will not work for the firm's owners unless it is in the managers' best interest. The agency problem is a result of the separation of the decision makers and the owners of the firm. As a result, managers may make decisions that are not in line with the goal of maximization of shareholder wealth.

F. **Avoiding Financial Crisis—Back to the Principles.** Many of the financial problems of the past can be traced back to ignoring the basic principles of finance.

G. **The Essential Elements of Ethics and Trust.** Ethical behavior is doing the right thing, and ethical dilemmas are everywhere in finance. Ethical behavior is important in financial management, just as it is important in everything we do. Unfortunately, precisely how we define what is and is not ethical behavior is sometimes difficult. Nevertheless, we should not give up the quest. In addition, business cannot interact unless they trust each other.

III. The Role of Finance in Business

A. There are three basic types of issues that are addressed by the study of finance.

1. **What long-term investments should the firm undertake?** This area of finance is generally referred to as capital budgeting.

2. **How should the firm raise money to fund these investments?** The firm's funding choices are generally referred to as capital structure decisions.

3. **How can the firm best manage its cash flows as they arise in its day-to-day operations?** This area of finance is generally referred to as working capital management.

IV. The Legal Forms of Business Organization

    A. The significance of different legal forms

        1. The predominant form of business organization in the United States in pure numbers is the sole proprietorship.

    B. **Sole proprietorship:** A business owned by a single person and that has a minimum amount of legal structure.

        1. Advantages

            a. Easily established with few complications

            b. Minimal organizational costs

            c. Does not have to share profits or control with others

        2. Disadvantages

            a. Unlimited liability for the owner

            b. Owner must absorb all losses

            c. Equity capital limited to the owner's personal investment

            d. Business terminates immediately upon death of owner

    C. **Partnership:** An association of two or more individuals coming together as co-owners to operate a business for profit.

        1. Two types of partnerships

            a. General partnership: Relationship between partners is dictated by the partnership agreement.

                (1) Advantages

                    (a) Minimal organizational requirements

                    (b) Negligible government regulations

                (2) Disadvantages

                    (a) All partners have unlimited liability.

                    (b) Difficult to raise large amounts of capital

                    (c) Partnership is dissolved by the death or withdrawal of the general partner.

b. Limited partnership

    (1) Advantages

        (a) For the limited partners, liability is limited to the amount of capital invested in the company.

        (b) Withdrawal or death of a limited partner does not affect continuity of the business.

        (c) Stronger inducement in raising capital

    (2) Disadvantages

        (a) There must be at least one general partner who has unlimited liability in the partnership.

        (b) Names of limited partners may not appear in the name of the firm.

        (c) Limited partners may not participate in the management of the business.

        (d) More expensive to organize than general partnership, as a written agreement is mandatory

D. **The corporation:** An "impersonal" legal entity that has the power to purchase, sell, and own assets and to incur liabilities while existing separately and apart from its owners.

    1. Ownership is evidenced by shares of stock.

    2. Advantages

        a. Limited liability of owners

        b. Ease of transferability of ownership (i.e., by the sale of one's shares of stock)

        c. The death of an owner does not result in the discontinuance of the firm's life.

        d. Ability to raise large amounts of capital

    3. Disadvantages

        a. Most difficult and expensive form of business to establish

        b. Control of corporation not guaranteed by partial ownership of stock

      c.   Corporations also suffer from a double taxation on dividends. The firm first pays taxes on the income it earns; after taxes have been paid on this income, it is returned to investors in the form of dividends. The investor then pays personal taxes on that dividend income.

4.   S-Type Corporations and Limited Liability Companies (LLC)

      a.   The S-type corporation provides limited liability while allowing the business owners to be taxed as if they were a partnership; that is, distributions back to the owners are not taxed twice as is the case with dividends in the corporate form.

      b.   The limited liability company (LLC) is a cross between a partnership and a corporation. The LLC retains limited liability for its owners, but runs and is taxed like a partnership.

<u>Self-Tests</u>

TRUE-FALSE

___F___ 1. The major problem with the goal of shareholder wealth maximization is that ignores the timing of the expected returns of the firm.

___T___ 2. Shareholder wealth maximization considers the effects of the riskiness of a prospective earnings stream.

___F___ 3. Many businesses are formed as corporations because of the ease of establishment.

___T___ 4. A sole proprietorship is a business owned by a single individual who maintains complete title to the assets and is also personally liable for all indebtedness incurred.

___T___ 5. Under a limited partnership, the limited partner's liability is limited to the amount of capital invested in the company.

___F___ 6. A limited liability company (LLC) is a cross between a partnership and a corporation, and the LLC retains limited liability for its owners, but runs and is taxed like a partnership.

___F___ 7. In general, the less risk a firm is willing to assume, the higher the expected return will be from a given course of action.

___F___ 8. Ethical considerations are not relevant in financial management.

___T___ 9. The agency problem is a result of the separation of the decision makers and the owners of the firm, and as a result, managers may make decisions that are not in line with the goal of maximization of shareholder wealth.

___F___ 10. In order to employ the goal of shareholder wealth maximization, every stock price change should be considered to be a market interpretation of the worth of our financial decisions.

___T___ 11. In measuring value we will use cash flows rather than accounting profits because it is only cash flows that the firm receives and is able to reinvest.

MULTIPLE CHOICE

1. The long-run goal of the firm is to

    a. hold large quantities of cash.
    b. increase sales regularly.
    c. maximize earnings per share.
    d. maximize shareholder wealth.

2. Maximizing shareholder wealth means maximizing the

    a. value of the firm's assets.
    b. value of the firm's cash.
    c. value of the firm's investments.
    d. value of the firm's profits.
    e. market value of the firm's common stock.

3. Advantages of the corporation include:

    a. transferability of ownership.
    b. unlimited liability.
    c. ability of the corporation to raise capital.
    d. double taxation of dividend income.
    e. a and c.
    f. a and b.

4. Disadvantages of the partnership are

    a. expense of formation.
    b. lack of permanence.
    c. double taxation on income.
    d. unlimited liability.
    e. b and d.
    f. a and d.

5. Profit maximization is not the proper objective of a firm because

    a. it is not as inclusive a goal as the maximization of shareholder wealth.
    b. it does not consider the uncertainty of the return.
    c. it does not consider the timing of the returns.
    d. All of the above are true.
    e. None of the above is true.

6.   The market price of a share of stock is determined by

     a.   the New York Stock Exchange.
     b.   the Federal Reserve.
     c.   the company's management.
     d.   individuals buying and selling the stock.

7.   Which of the following forms of business organization is the largest in number?

     a.   corporation
     b.   partnership
     c.   sole proprietorship

8.   The agency problem

     a.   is associated with insuring the firm.
     b.   is no longer important.
     c.   invalidates the goal of maximization of shareholder wealth.
     d.   is a result of the separation of the decision makers and the owners of the firm.
     e.   is all of the above.

CHAPTER 2

The Financial Markets
and Interest Rates

Orientation: This chapter considers the market environment in which long-term capital is raised. The underlying rationale for the existence of security markets is presented, investment banking services and procedures are detailed, private placements are discussed, and security market regulations are reviewed. Further discussions cover rates of return over long periods and recent periods, interest rate determinants, and theories of the term structure of interest rates.

I.   Components of the U.S. Financial Market System

    A.   *Public offerings* can be distinguished from *private placements*.

        1.   The public (financial) market is an impersonal market in which both individual and institutional investors have the opportunity to acquire securities.

            a.   A public offering takes place in the public market.

            b.   The security-issuing firm does not meet (face-to-face) the actual investors in the securities.

        2.   In a private placement of securities, only a limited number of investors have the opportunity to purchase a portion of the issue.

            a.   The market for private placements is more personal than its public counterpart.

            b.   The specific details of the issue may actually be developed on a face-to-face basis among the potential investors and the issuer.

B. Private placements and venture capital

    1. Private placements can involve issuing both debt and equity, and "venture capitalists" can play an active role in both.

    2. For startup companies or companies in the early stages of business, as well as firms in "turnaround" situations, venture capital is a prime source of funds. The venture capitalist firm will frequently acquire a meaningful dollar state in the startup firm.

C. *Primary markets* can be distinguished from *secondary markets*.

    1. Securities are first offered for sale in a primary market. For example, the sale of a new bond issue, preferred stock issue, or common stock issue takes place in the primary market. These transactions increase the total stock of financial assets in existence in the economy.

    2. Trading in currently existing securities takes place in the secondary market. The total stock of financial assets is unaffected by such transactions.

D. The *money market* can be distinguished from the *capital market*.

    1. The money market consists of the institutions and procedures that provide for transactions in short-term debt instruments, which are generally issued by borrowers who have very high credit ratings.

        a. "Short-term" means that the securities traded in the money market have maturity periods of not more than one year.

        b. Equity instruments are not traded in the money market.

        c. Typical examples of money market instruments are (1) U.S. Treasury bills, (2) federal agency securities, (3) bankers' acceptances, (4) negotiable certificates of deposit, and (5) commercial paper.

    2. The capital market consists of the institutions and procedures that provide for transactions in long-term financial instruments. This market encompasses those securities that have maturity periods extending beyond one year.

E.   *Spot markets* can be distinguished from *futures markets.*

1.   Cash markets are where something sells today, right now, on the spot; in fact, cash markets are often referred to as "spot" markets.

2.   Futures markets are where you can set a price to buy or sell something at some future date; in effect, you sign a contract that states what you're buying, how much of it you're buying, at what price you're buying it, and when you will actually make the purchase.

F.   *Organized security exchanges* can be distinguished from *over-the-counter markets.*

1.   Organized security exchanges are tangible entities whose activities are governed by a set of bylaws. Security exchanges physically occupy space, and financial instruments are traded on such premises.

a.   Major stock exchanges must comply with a strict set of reporting requirements established by the Securities and Exchange Commission (SEC). These exchanges are said to be *registered.*

b.   Organized security exchanges provide several benefits to both corporations and investors. They (1) provide a continuous market, (2) establish and publicize fair security prices, and (3) help businesses raise new financial capital.

c.   A corporation must take steps to have its securities *listed* on an exchange in order to directly receive the benefits noted above. Listing criteria differ from exchange to exchange.

2.   Over-the-counter markets include all security markets *except* the organized exchanges. The money market is a prominent example. Most corporate bonds are traded over the counter.

II.   Using an Investment Banker

A.   The investment banker is a financial specialist who acts as an intermediary in the selling of securities. He or she works for an investment banking firm (house).

B.   The investment banker provides three basic functions.

1.   He or she assumes the risk of selling a new security issue at a satisfactory (profitable) price. This is called *underwriting.* Typically, the investment banking house, along with the

underwriting syndicate, actually buys the new issue from the corporation that is raising funds. The syndicate (group of investment banking firms) then sells the issue to the investing public at a higher price (hopefully) than it paid for it.

2.   He or she provides for the *distribution* of the securities to the investing public.

3.   He or she *advises* firms on the details of selling securities.

C.   Several distribution methods are available for placing new securities into the hands of final investors. The investment banker's role is different in each case.

1.   In a *negotiated purchase*, the firm in need of funds contacts an investment banker and begins the sequence of steps leading to the final distribution of the securities that will be offered. The price that the investment banker pays for the securities is "negotiated" with the issuing firm.

2.   In a *competitive-bid purchase*, the investment banker and underwriting syndicate are selected by an auction process. The syndicate willing to pay the greatest dollar amount per new security to the issuing firm wins the competitive bid. This means that it will underwrite and distribute the issue. In this situation, the price paid to the issuer is not negotiated; instead, it is determined by a sealed-bid process much on the order of construction bids.

3.   In a *commission* (or *best-efforts*) offering, the investment banker does not act as an underwriter. He or she attempts to sell the issue in return for a fixed commission on each security that is actually sold. Unsold securities are simply returned to the firm hoping to raise funds.

4.   In a *privileged subscription*, the new issue is not offered to the investing public. It is sold to a definite and limited group of investors. Current stockholders are often the privileged group.

5.   In a *Dutch auction,* investors first put in bids giving the number of shares they would like to buy and the price they are willing to pay for them. Once the bids are in, they are ranked, and the selling price is calculated as the highest price that allows for all the stock to be sold.

6. In a *direct sale*, the issuing firm sells the securities to the investing public without involving an investment banker in the process. This is not a typical procedure.

D. The negotiated purchase is most likely to be the distribution method used by the private corporation. It consists of several steps.

1. The security-issuing firm selects an investment banker.

2. A series of pre-underwriting conferences takes place. Discussions center on: (1) the amount of capital to be raised; (2) the possible receptiveness of the capital markets to a specific mode of financing; and (3) the proposed use of the new funds. These conferences are consummated by the signing of a *tentative underwriting agreement*. The approximate price to be paid for each security is identified in this agreement.

3. An underwriting syndicate is formed. The syndicate is a temporary association of investment bankers formed to purchase the security issue from the corporation. The syndicate's objective is to resell the issue at a profit.

4. Most new public issues must be registered with the SEC before they can be sold to final investors. This involves filing a lengthy technical document called a *registration statement* with the SEC. This document aims to disclose relevant facts about the issuing firm and the related security to potential investors. Another document, the *prospectus*, is also filed with the SEC for examination. It is a shortened version of the official registration statement. Once both documents are approved, the prospectus becomes the official advertising vehicle for the security offering.

5. A selling group is formed to distribute the new securities to final investors. Securities dealers who are part of the selling group are permitted to purchase a portion of the new issue at a price to the public. A *selling-group agreement* binds the syndicate and the members of the selling group.

6. A due-diligence meeting is held to finalize all details prior to taking the offering to the public. The price at which the issuing firm will sell the new securities to the syndicate is settled. Usually, the offering is made to the public on the day after this meeting.

7. The syndicate manager (from the investment banking house that generated the business) is permitted to mitigate downward price

movements in the secondary market for the subject offering. This is accomplished by the syndicate managers placing buy orders for the security at the agreed-upon public offering price.

8.   A contractual agreement among the syndicate members terminates the syndicate. In the most pleasant situations, this agreement is made when the issue is fully subscribed (sold).

III.   Private Placements

A.   Each year, billions of dollars of new securities are privately (directly) placed with final investors. In a private placement, a small number of investors purchase the entire security offering. Most private placements involve debt instruments.

B.   Large financial institutions are the major investors in private placements. These include (1) life insurance firms, (2) state and local retirement funds, and (3) private pension funds.

C.   The advantages and disadvantages of private placements as opposed to public offerings must be carefully evaluated by management.

1.   The advantages include (1) greater speed than a public offering in actually obtaining the needed funds, (2) lower flotation costs than are associated with a public issue, and (3) increased flexibility in the financing contract.

2.   The disadvantages include (1) higher interest costs than are ordinarily associated with a comparable public issue, (2) the imposition of several restrictive covenants in the financing contract, and (3) the possibility that the security may have to be registered some time in the future at the lender's option.

IV.   Flotation Costs

A.   The firm raising long-term capital typically incurs two types of flotation costs: (1) the underwriter's spread and (2) issuing costs. The former is typically the larger.

1.   The underwriter's spread is the difference between the gross and net proceeds from a specific security issue. This absolute dollar difference is usually expressed as a percent of the gross proceeds.

2.   Many components comprise issue costs. The two most significant are (1) printing and engraving and (2) legal fees. For comparison

purposes, these are usually expressed as a percent of the issue's gross proceeds.

B. SEC data reveal two relationships about flotation costs.

    1. Issue costs (as a percent of gross proceeds) for common stock exceed those of preferred stock, which exceed those of bonds.

    2. Total flotation costs per dollar raised decrease as the dollar size of the security issue increases.

V. Regulation Aimed at Making the Goal of the Firm Work

A. In July 2002, Congress passed the Public Company Accounting Reform and Investor Protection Act. The short name for the act became the *Sarbanes-Oxley Act of 2002*.

    1. The Sarbanes-Oxley Act was passed as the result of a large series of corporate indiscretions.

    2. The act holds corporate advisors (like accountants, lawyers, company officers, and boards of directors) who have access to or influence company decisions strictly accountable in a legal sense for any instances of misconduct.

VI. Observed Rates of Return in the Financial Markets

A. Ibbotson Associates examined the realized rates of return for a wide variety of securities over the period from 1926 to 2003. They have found the following:

    1. The average inflation rate (the "inflation-risk premium") has been about 3.2 percent annually.

    2. The default-risk premium for long-term corporate bonds over long-term government bonds has between about 1.0 percent annually.

    3. Large common stocks earned 5.5 percent more than the rate earned on long-term corporate bonds, and small firms earned 5.7 percent more than the average annual return on large firms.

VII. Interest Rate Determinants

A. The real rate of interest is the difference in the nominal rate and the anticipated rate of inflation.

B.   The notion of a real rate of interest can be thought of as the "price for deferring consumption."

C.   Letting the nominal rate of interest be represented by k_{rf}, the anticipated rate of inflation by IRP, and the real rate of interest by k^*, we can express the result by the following equation:

$$1 + \text{real rate of interest} = (1 + \text{nominal rate of interest})(1 + \text{anticipated rate of inflation})$$

or   real rate of interest = nominal rate of interest + anticipated rate of inflation + (anticipated rate of inflation)(nominal rate of interest)

For example, if the real rate is 5% and the expected inflation rate is 4%, the real rate would then be 9.2%, computed as follows:

$$\text{real rate of interest} = .05 + .04 + (.05)(.04)$$
$$= .092 \text{ or } 9.2\%$$

VIII.   The Term Structure of Interest Rates

A.   The relationship between a debt security's rate of return and the length of time until the debt matures is known as the *term structure of interest rates*.

B.   The term structure reflects observed rates or yields on similar securities, except for the length of time until maturity, at a particular moment in time.

C.   Three theories have been suggested to explain the term structure of interest rates.

1.   The **unbiased expectations theory** says that the term structure is determined by an investor's expectations about future interest rates.

2.   The **liquidity preference theory** suggests that investors require liquidity premiums (additional returns) to compensate them for buying securities which expose them to a greater risk of fluctuating interest rates.

3.   The **market segmentation theory** is built on the notion that legal restrictions and personal preferences limit investment choices to certain ranges of maturities and, therefore, affect the rates of return required in each range.

IX   Multinational Firm and Intercountry Risk

A.   Underdeveloped countries lack effective financial market systems.

B.   Multinational firms with cash to invest in foreign markets will not consider markets in which financial systems or political environments are uncertain or unstable.

Study Problem

1. If the expected inflation rate is 4%, and the real rate of interest is 8%, what is the nominal interest rate?

   SOLUTION

   $$\text{Nominal rate, } k_{rf} = \left(\begin{array}{c}\text{Real} \\ \text{rate}\end{array}\right) + \left(\begin{array}{c}\text{Inflation} \\ \text{rate}\end{array}\right) + \left(\begin{array}{c}\text{Real} \\ \text{rate}\end{array}\right)\left(\begin{array}{c}\text{Inflation} \\ \text{rate}\end{array}\right)$$

   $$= .08 + .04 + (.08)(.04)$$
   $$= .1232 = 12.32\%$$

Self Tests

TRUE-FALSE

_____ 1. A share of IBM common stock is a real asset.

_____ 2. Capital formation in underdeveloped countries might be assisted if those countries' financial market systems were more extensively developed.

_____ 3. General Motors is a typical example of a financial intermediary.

_____ 4. The Money Market is housed at 11 Wall Street, New York City.

_____ 5. Common stocks are money market instruments.

_____ 6. Price quotations on organized security exchanges have been facilitated by the existence of NASDAQ.

_____ 7. The cash market is also called the "spot" market.

_____ 8. In a negotiated purchase, the price the investment banker pays the security-issuing firm for the new issue is negotiated between these parties.

_____ 9. The futures market and the spot market are the same.

_____ 10. Life insurance companies are major purchasers of privately placed securities.

_____ 11. Secondary markets reduce the risk of investing in financial claims.

_____ 12. Equity instruments are traded in the money market.

_____ 13. The capital market includes those securities that have maturity periods extending beyond one year.

_____ 14. Trading in currently existing securities takes place in the primary market.

_____ 15. When new funds are being raised in a typical year, corporate equity markets are favored over corporate debt markets, in terms of dollar volume.

_____ 16. The U.S. tax system favors debt as a method of raising capital in comparison to equity instruments.

_____ 17. A life insurance company is an example of a financial intermediary.

_____ 18. "Market Segmentation Theory" refers to the use of debt versus the use of common stock to raise new funds.

_____ 19. Flotation costs for debt generally exceed those of common stock.

_____ 20. In general, the underwriter's spread component of flotation costs exceeds the issuing costs.

_____ 21. Inventories represent a category of financial assets.

_____ 22. Financial markets allocate savings in the economy to demanders of those funds.

_____ 23. Financial intermediaries issue their own financial claims, called direct securities, and then invest the money obtained in indirect securities, the financial claims of other economic units.

_____ 24. The U.S. government is the largest savings-surplus sector in the economy.

_____ 25. Financial markets provide a mechanism to facilitate the transfer of savings from those economic units that have a savings surplus to those that have a savings deficit.

_____ 26. The New York Stock Exchange, American Stock Exchange, and Midwest Stock Exchange are the only three *national* exchanges in the U.S.

_____ 27. There is an inverse relationship between the total flotation cost per dollar of funds raised and the amount of the security issue.

_____ 28. The primary objective of the Securities Act of 1933 is to provide potential investors with accurate and truthful disclosure about the firm and the new securities being sold.

_____ 29. Long-term corporate bonds are more risky than common stocks from the investor's point of view.

MULTIPLE CHOICE

1. Which of the following is *not* a benefit provided by the existence of organized security exchanges?

   a. a continuous market
   b. helping business raise new capital
   c. keeping long-term bond prices below 8 percent
   d. establishing and publicizing fair security prices

2. What is it called when an investment banker agrees to sell only as many securities as he or she can at an established price?

   a. a private placement
   b. a direct placement
   c. a privileged subscription
   d. a best-efforts agreement
   e. an upset agreement

3. Which of the following security distribution methods is least profitable to the investment banker?

   a. negotiated purchase
   b. competitive-bid purchase
   c. commission basis
   d. privileged subscription
   e. direct sale

4. A prospectus most closely resembles

   a. a registration statement.
   b. a red herring.
   c. a selling group agreement.
   d. a letter of credit.

5.   The purpose of financial markets is to

   a.   lower bond yields.
   b.   allocate savings efficiently.
   c.   raise stock prices.
   d.   employ stock brokers.

6.   The maturity boundary dividing the U.S. money and capital markets is

   a.   an arbitrary classification system.
   b.   set by the Federal Reserve Board.
   c.   periodically reviewed and altered by the SEC.
   d.   determined by the U.S. Treasury.

7.   Flotation costs are highest on

   a.   bonds.
   b.   preferred stock.
   c.   common stock.

8.   The spot market is
   a.   the same as the futures market.
   b.   the same as the underwriting market.
   c.   the same as the venture capital market.
   d.   the same as the cash market.

9.   Which of the following methods for the distribution of securities bypasses the use of an investment banker?

   a.   negotiated purchase
   b.   competitive-bid purchase
   c.   direct sales
   d.   best-efforts basis
   e.   privileged subscriptions

10.   The difference between the gross and net proceeds from a given security issue expressed as a percent of the gross proceeds is known as

   a.   issue costs.
   b.   flotation costs.
   c.   underwriter's spread.
   d.   legal fees.

11.   Which of the following is generally *not* an advantage of private placements?

    a. speed
    b. reduced flotation costs
    c. financing flexibility
    d. interest costs

12.   Which of the following is *not* an example of a money market instrument?

    a. U.S. Treasury bills
    b. common stock
    c. federal agency securities
    d. commercial paper

13.   An agreement that obligates the investment banker to underwrite securities that are not accepted by privileged investors is known as a

    a. privileged subscription.
    b. standby agreement.
    c. negotiated purchase.
    d. best-efforts basis.

14.   _____ is the interest rate paid on debt securities without adjusting for loss in purchasing power.

    a. Real risk-free interest rate
    b. Risk-free rate
    c. Nominal rate
    d. Risk premium
    e. Inflation rate

15.   Insurance companies invest in the "long-end" of the securities market. In which of the following instruments would an insurance company be *least* likely to invest *most* of its funds?

    a. mortgages
    b. corporate bonds
    c. commercial paper
    d. corporate stocks

16.   Which of the following is/are NYSE listing requirements?

    a.   profitability
    b.   market value
    c.   public ownership
    d.   All of the above are requirements.
    e.   None of the above are requirements.

17.   The indirect method of transferring savings in which securities are not transformed, but passed through to other purchasers, most frequently involves

    a.   an established relationship between buyer and issuer.
    b.   a finance company.
    c.   a commercial bank.
    d.   an investment banker.
    e.   all of the above.

18.   Which of the following does not describe an organized security exchange?

    a.   It occupies physical space as opposed to being strictly communication links among traders.
    b.   It is strictly regional in scope.
    c.   It is regulated by the Securities and Exchange Commission.
    d.   Its trades are conducted strictly by exchange members.

19.   A seasoned equity offering or SEO is
    a.   illegal in Canada.
    b.   is also called an inverse IPO.
    c.   is the same as an IPO.
    d.   the sale of additional shares by a company whose shares are already publicly traded.

20.   Primary markets are distinguished from secondary markets by the fact that

    a.   primary markets sell securities for corporations with assets over $2 million, while secondary markets sell securities for corporations with assets less than $2 million.
    b.   primary markets are more developed than the secondary markets.
    c.   primary markets trade new securities issues while secondary markets trade existing securities.
    d.   primary markets enjoy higher trading volume than the secondary markets do.

21.   How many registered stock exchanges are there in the United States?

    a.   four
    b.   five
    c.   more than five
    d.   none

22.   What is the correct *sequence* of steps for the negotiated purchase distribution method? The key steps follow each Roman numeral, below.

    I.   File a registration statement and prospectus with SEC.
    II.   Hold a due diligence meeting.
    III.   Form an underwriting syndicate.
    IV.   Form a contractual agreement among syndicate members to terminate the syndicate.
    V.   Form a selling group to distribute new securities.

    a.   I, II, III, IV, V
    b.   II, III, I, V, IV
    c.   III, I, V, II, IV
    d.   IV, I, II, III, V

23.   Under a Dutch Auction,
    a.   you know ahead of time how many shares you will get.
    b.   you know ahead of time at what price you will get the shares.
    c.   the final price set that fills the quota of shares to sell becomes the offering price to all successful bidders.
    d.   the shares must be sold in Holland.

24.   In terms of risk, it is correct to say:

    a.   Government securities are less risky than common stocks, but more risky than corporate bonds.
    b.   Corporate bonds are less risky than common stocks.
    c.   Long-term government securities are less risky than short-term government securities.
    d.   Common stocks of large companies are more risky than the common stocks of small firms.

25.   The term structure of interest rates refers to

   a.   the different risk levels of interest rates.
   b.   the different interest rates of securities with the same maturity dates.
   c.   the different interest rates of securities with the same risk but with different maturity dates.
   d.   the terms of agreement associated with a bond's interest payments.

CHAPTER 3

Understanding Financial Statements and Cash Flows

<u>Orientation:</u> In this chapter, we review the contents and meaning of a firm's income statement and balance sheet. We also look very carefully at how to compute a firm's cash flows.

I.   Basic Financial Statements

    A.   The Income Statement

        1.   The income statement reports the results from operating the business for a period of time, such as a year.

        2.   It is helpful to think of the income statement as comprising four types of activities.

            a.   Selling the product

            b.   The cost of producing or acquiring the goods or services sold

            c.   The expenses incurred in marketing and distributing the product or service to the customer, along with administrative operating expenses

            d.   The financing costs of doing business, for example, interest paid to creditors and dividend payments to the preferred stockholders

B.   The Balance Sheet

    1.   The balance sheet provides a snapshot of the firm's financial position at a specific point in time, presenting its asset holdings, liabilities, and owner-supplied capital.

        a.   Assets represent the resources owned by the firm.

            1.   Current assets—consisting primarily of cash, marketable securities, accounts receivable, inventories, and prepaid expenses

            2.   Fixed or long-term assets—comprising equipment, buildings, and land

            3.   Other assets—all assets not otherwise included in the firm's current assets or fixed assets, such as patents, long-term investments in securities, and goodwill

        b.   The liabilities and owners' equity indicate how those resources are financed.

            1.   The debt consists of such sources as credit extended from suppliers or a loan from a bank.

            2.   The equity includes the stockholders' investment in the firm and the cumulative profits retained in the business up to the date of the balance sheet.

    2.   The balance sheet is not intended to represent the current market value of the company but rather reports the historical transactions recorded at their cost.

C.   Statement of Cash Flows

    1.   While an income statement measures a company's profits, profits are not the same as cash flows; profits are calculated on an *accrual* basis rather than a *cash* basis.

    2.   The basic format of a statement of cash flows is as follows:

Cash flows from operations
+/-   cash flows from investing activities
+/-   cash flows from financing activities
=   change in cash
+   beginning cash
=   ending cash

3.   Thus, we can explain all the cash inflows and outflows of a business by looking at three activities.

    a.   *Generating cash flows from day-to-day business operations.* **Cash flows from operations** equals:

Net income
+   Depreciation expense
−   additional uncollected sales (increase in accounts receivables) and
−   cash payments for inventories (increases in inventories less increases in accounts payables)

    b.   *Investing in fixed assets and other long-term assets.* When a company purchases fixed assets, such as equipment or buildings, these expenditures are shown as an increase in *gross* fixed assets (not the increase in *net* fixed assets) in the balance sheet. Also, as part of investment activities, we must recognize any changes (increases or decreases) in any other assets.

Cash flows from investing activities are determined as follows

−   increase in *gross* fixed assets (cash outflow)
−   increase in other assets (cash outflow)

or

+   decrease in gross fixed assets (cash inflows)
+   decrease in other assets (cash inflow)

c.   *Financing the business.* Financing a business involves (1) paying dividends to the owners; (2) increasing or decreasing short-term and long-term debt, which means borrowing more money (an increase in debt) or paying off debt (a decrease in debt); and (3) selling shares of stock (source of cash) or repurchasing stock (use of cash). A firm's **cash flows from financing activities** are equal to:

+   increase in interest-bearing debt (cash inflow)

or

−   decrease in interest-bearing debt (cash outflow)

+   increase in common stock (cash inflow)

or

−   decrease in common stock (cash outflow)

−   dividend payments (cash outflow)

II.   Federal Income Taxation for a Corporation

A.   Taxable income is basically determined as income less allowable exclusions and tax-deductible expenses.

B.   Interest expense is a tax-deductible expense; however, dividends paid by a corporation to its stockholders are not a tax-deductible expense.

C.   Corporate rate structure:

15%	$0	−	$50,000
25%	$50,001	−	$75,000
34%	$75,001	−	$10,000,000
35%	over		$10,000,000

There is an additional surtax of 5 percent for income between $100,000 and $335,000.

There is also an additional surtax of 3 percent on income between $15 million and $18.3 million.

Study Problems

1. Prepare a balance sheet for the A. R. Peterson Mfg. Co. from the scrambled list of items below. The owner's equity balance is not given, but it can be determined as a balancing figure.

Building	$49,100	Office equipment	4,100
Accounts receivable	21,600	Land	22,000
Machinery	2,950	Notes payable	14,000
Cash	9,200	Owners' equity	
Accounts payable	16,500		

SOLUTION

A. R. Peterson Mfg. Co.
Balance Sheet

Cash	$ 9,200	Accounts payable	16,500
Accounts receivable	21,600	Notes payable	14,000
Land	22,000	Owner's equity	78,450
Building	49,100		
Machinery	2,950		
Office equipment	4,100	Total liabilities	
Total assets	$108,950	& owners' equity	$108,950

2. By studying the successive balance sheets for AMP, Inc. found below, determine what transactions have occurred. Prepare a list of the transactions and the corresponding balance-sheet dates. For example, on March 31, 2010, the firm's owners invested $200,000 in AMP, Inc. and started the business.

(a)

AMP, Inc.
Balance Sheet
March 31, 2010

Assets		Owners' Equity	
Cash	$200,000	Owners' equity	$200,000

(b)

AMP, Inc.
Balance Sheet
April 2, 2010

Assets		Owners' Equity	
Cash	$100,000	Owners' equity	$200,000
Land	100,000		
	$200,000		$200,000

(c)

AMP, Inc.
Balance Sheet
April 15, 2010

Assets		Owners' Equity	
Cash	$ 50,000	Owners' equity	$200,000
Building	50,000		
Land	100,000		
	$200,000		$200,000

(d)

AMP, Inc.
Balance Sheet
May 2, 2010

Assets		Liabilities & Owners' Equity	
Cash	$50,000	Accounts payable	$25,000
Inventories	25,000	Owners' equity	200,000
Building	50,000		
Land	100,000		
	$225,000		$225,000

(e)

AMP, Inc.
Balance Sheet
May 15, 2010

Assets		Liabilities & Owners' Equity	
Cash	$60,000	Accounts payable	$25,000
Inventories	25,000	Notes payable	25,000
Equipment	15,000	Owners' equity	200,000
Building	50,000		
Land	100,000		
	$250,000		$250,000

SOLUTION

(a) On March 31, the firm's owners invested $200,000 in AMP, Inc. and started the business.

(b) On April 2, $100,000 of the original investment by the owners was used to acquire land.

(c) On April 15, $50,000 of the original cash was used to acquire a building.

(d) On May 2, $25,000 of inventory was purchased on account (credit).

(e) On May 15, a $25,000 loan was obtained and $15,000 of the proceeds used to purchase equipment.

3.   Burruss, Inc. had the following condensed balance sheet at the end of operation for 2009:

Burruss, Inc.
Balance Sheet
December 31, 2009

Cash	$ 54,000	Accounts payable	$ 20,000
Accounts receivable	20,000	Short-term notes	10,000
Inventory	31,000	Total short-term debt	$30,000
Total current assets	$ 75,000	Long-term debt	73,000
Fixed assets (net)	125,000	Common stock	150,000
Land	62,000	Retained earnings	49,000
Investments	10,000		
	$302,000		$302,000

In the following year, 2010, the following activities occurred.

(a)   Burruss, Inc. made long-term investments of $ 10,000.

(b)   Additional land for a plant expansion was purchased for $12,000.

(c)   Long-term debt was reduced in the amount of $2,000.

(d)   An additional $20,000 in common stock was issued.

(e)   Dividends of $15,000 were paid to stockholders.

(f)   Net income for 2010 was $42,000 after allowing for $18,000 in depreciation.

(g)   The firm paid $25,000 in income taxes.

(h)   Interest expense was $10,000.

(i)   A second parcel of land was purchased for $18,000 through the issuance of long-term notes.

(j)   Accounts receivable and inventory increased $10,000 and $15,000, respectively, while accounts payable increased $10,000.

(k)   Short-term notes remained unchanged.

Required:

(a) Prepare a balance sheet for Burruss, Inc. at December 31, 2010. (You will be able to determine all the items in the 2010 balance sheet except cash. But since it will be the only item not mentioned, it will simply be the amount that makes total assets equal to total debt and equity.).

(b) Compute the firm's cash flows for 2010.

SOLUTION

Burruss, Inc.
Balance Sheet
December 31, 2010

Cash	$ 80,000	Accounts payable	$ 30,000
Accounts receivable	30,000	Short-term notes	10,000
Inventory	46,000	Total current liabilities	$40,000
Total Current Assets	$156,000	Long-term debt	89,000
Fixed assets (net)	107,000	Common stock	170,000
Land	92,000	Retained earnings	76,000
Investments	20,000		
Total	$375,000		$375,000

Burruss, Inc.
Statement of Cash Flows
For the Year Ended December 31, 2010

Cash flow from operations:		
Net income		$ 42,000
Plus depreciation		18,000
Increase in account receivable		($10,000)
Cash payments on inventory:		
Increase in inventory	($15,000)	
Less increase in accounts payables	10,000	($5,000)
Cash flows from operations		$45,000
Investment activities:		
Change in fixed assets	$0	
Increase in land	(30,000)	
Increase in investments	(10,000)	
Total investment activities		($40,000)

Financing activities:

Dividends	(15,000)	
Decrease in long-term debt[i]	16,000	
Increase in common stock	20,000	
Total financing activities		$21,000
Change in cash flows		$18,000
Beginning cash		54,000
Ending cash		$72,000

4. Financial statements are provided below for the Dalton Corporation. Compute the firm's cash flows for 2010.

ASSETS

	12/31/2009	12/31/2010
CURRENT ASSETS		
Cash	$ 19,606	$ 166,594
Accounts Receivable	138,021	186,829
TOTAL CURRENT ASSETS	$ 157,628	$ 353,423
FIXED ASSETS		
Trucks	$ 97,529	$ 124,949
Equipment	94,748	135,833
Accumulated Depreciation	(112,516)	(146,945)
TOTAL FIXED ASSETS	$ 79,761	$ 113,837
TOTAL ASSETS	$ 237,388	$ 467,260

LIABILITIES AND EQUITY

CURRENT LIABILITIES		
Accruals	$ 12,600	$ 14,300
Short-term notes	49,810	119,281
Total current liabilities	$ 62,410	$ 133,581
EQUITY:		
Common stock	$ 146,944	$ 146,944
Retained earnings	28,034	186,735
TOTAL EQUITY	$ 174,978	$ 333,679
TOTAL LIABILITIES AND EQUITY	$ 237,388	$ 467,260

---

[i] $16,000 = $18,000 increase in long-term debt to buy land less $2,000 reduction in long-term notes.

	12/31/2010
Sales	$ 1,824,568
Cost of goods sold	$ 649,214
Gross profit	$ 1,175,354
Operating expenses	
Selling, general & admin. expenses	861,816
Depreciation expense	34,429
Operating income	$ 279,109
Interest expense	8,205
Earnings before taxes	$ 270,904
Taxes	105,653
Net income	$ 165,252

SOLUTION

Cash flows from operations:

Net income	$ 165,252
Plus depreciation	34,429
Increase in accounts receivable	(48,808)
Increase in accruals	1,700
Cash flows from operations	$152,573

| Increase in gross fixed assets | ($68,505) |

Financing activities:

Dividends	($6,551)
Increase in short-term notes	69,472
Change in cash	$146,989
Beginning cash	19,606
Ending cash	$166,595

5.   A corporation had $145,000 in taxable earnings. What is the tax liability?

SOLUTION

Income		Marginal Tax Rate		Tax Liability
$ 50,000	x	15%		$ 7,500
25,000	x	25%		6,250
25,000	x	34%		8,500
45,000	x	39%		17,550
$145,000		Total tax liability	=	$39,800

6.   A corporation has earnings before interest and taxes of $86,000, dividend expense of $8,000, and interest expenses of $9,000. What is the corporation's (a) taxable income and (b) tax liability?

SOLUTION

(a)   Operating income $87,600

       Interest expense   (9,000)

       Contribution   (1,000)

       Taxable income $77,600

(b)   15%   x $50,000   = $ 7,500

       25%   x   25,000   =   6,250

       34%   x   2,600   =   884

                 $77,600 $14,634   =   Tax liability

7.   The M. M. Roscoe Corporation is a regional truck dealer. The firm sells new and used trucks and is actively involved in the parts business. During the most recent year, the company generated sales of $4 million. The combined cost of goods sold and the operating expenses were $3.2 million. Also, $268,500 in interest expense was paid during the year. Calculate the corporation's tax liability.

SOLUTION

M.M. Roscoe Corp.—Corporate Income Tax

Sales	$4,000,000
Cost of goods sold + operating expenses	(3,200,000)
Operating profits	$800,000
Interest expense	(268,500)
Taxable ordinary income	$531,500

Tax liability:

$50,000 x .15 =	$7,500
25,000 x .25 =	6,250
456,500 x .34 =	155,210
Surtax:	
$235,000 x .05 =	11,750
Total taxes due =	$180,710

Self-Tests

TRUE-FALSE

_____ 1. The balance sheet is a statement of the firm's financial position over a specified time interval.

_____ 2. Non-current assets are those that are not expected to be converted into cash within the firm's operating cycle.

_____ 3. The income statement represents an attempt to measure the net results of the firm's operations on a given date.

_____ 4. The owner's equity represents the book value of the owner's investment in the assets of the firm.

_____ 5. A firm attempts to match sales from the period's operations with the expenses incurred in generating those revenues by compiling the income statement on an accrual basis.

_____ 6. Reported sales and expenses must represent actual cash flows for the period when the income statement is prepared on an accrual basis.

_____ 7. Investments in securities are always considered to be current assets.

_____ 8. Cash flows from operations are equal to a firm's operating income plus depreciation and amortization.

_____ 9. Current liabilities include accounts payables and accruals.

_____ 10. Depreciation expense is added back to net income when computing after-tax cash flows from operations because it is a non-cash expense.

_____ 11. Interest expense is an operating expense.

_____ 12. Retained earnings change is affected by a firm's net income and common stock dividends paid.

MULTIPLE CHOICE

1. Which of the following is generally considered to be the most important for judging the economic well-being of a firm?

   a. income statement
   b. assets and liabilities
   c. cash flows
   d. all of the above
   e. none of the above

2. Which Income Statement activity is not found above the Operating Profit line?

   a. financing
   b. operating expenses
   c. revenue
   d. cost of acquiring the product or service

3. Which type of income may be distributed to the company's owners or reinvested in the company?

   a. gross profit
   b. net income
   c. operating income
   d. earnings before preferred dividends

4. The balance sheet provides us with

   a. how the company's resources are financed.
   b. the results from operating the business for a period of time.
   c. the result of all financial transactions since the company began its operations.
   d. both a and c.

5. Which item is not considered a liability?

   a. credit extended by suppliers to a firm for the purchase of inventory
   b. interest payable
   c. accrued taxes
   d. prepaid rent

6.   Common Stockholders' Equity equals:

    a.   common stock issued, plus treasury stock, plus retained earnings.

    b.   common stock issued, minus common stock repurchased, plus cumulative net income over the firm's life, minus taxes and total dividends paid over the firm's life.

    c.   preferred stock issued plus common stock issued, minus treasury stock, plus retained earnings.

    d.   common stock issued, minus common stock repurchased, plus retained earnings.

7.   Which item below is not considered a difference between accrual-basis and cash-basis accounting?

    a.   depreciation expense

    b.   the accounting treatment of employees' salaries that are paid on a bi-weekly basis

    c.   credit purchases of inventory

    d.   cash sales, as opposed to credit

8.   Which item listed below is not part of the calculation of net working capitals?

    a.   long-term notes payable

    b.   accounts payable

    c.   accounts receivable

    d.   prepaid expenses

9.   Which of the following is not considered to be a financing activity?

    a.   dividend payments

    b.   issuing stock

    c.   purchase of a capital asset

    d.   paying off debt

CHAPTER 4

Evaluating a Firm's Financial Performance

<u>Orientation</u>: Financial analysis can be defined as the process of assessing the financial condition of a firm. The principal analytical tool of the financial analyst is the financial ratio. This chapter provides a set of key financial ratios and a discussion of their effective use.

I   Financial ratios help us identify some of the financial strengths and weaknesses of a company.

II.   The ratios give us a way of making meaningful comparisons of a firm's financial data at different points in time and with other firms.

III.   We could use ratios to answer the following important questions about a firm's operations.

    A.   **Question 1: How liquid is the firm?**

        1.   The liquidity of a business is defined as its ability to meet maturing debt obligations. That is, does or will the firm have the resources to pay the creditors when the debt comes due?

        2.   There are two ways to approach the liquidity question.

            a.   We can look at the firm's assets that are relatively liquid in nature and compare them to the amount of the debt coming due in the near term.

            b.   We can look at how quickly the firm's liquid assets are being converted into cash.

B. **Question 2: Is management generating adequate operating profits on the firm's assets?**

1. We want to know if the profits are sufficient relative to the assets being invested.

2. We have several choices as to how we measure profits: gross profits, operating profits, or net income. Gross profits are not acceptable because it overlooks important information such as marketing and distribution expenses. Net income includes the unwanted effects of the firm's financing policies. This leaves operating profits as our best choice in measuring the firm's operating profitability. Thus, the appropriate measure is the operating return on assets (OROA):

$$\text{OROA} = \frac{\text{operating profits}}{\text{total assets}}.$$

C. **Question 3: How is the firm financing its assets?**

Here we are concerned with the mix of debt and equity capital the firm is using. Two primary ratios used to answer this question are the debt ratio and times interest earned. The debt ratio is the proportion of total debt to total assets. Times interest earned compares operating profits to interest expense for a crude measure of the firm's capacity to service its debt.

D. **Question 4: Are the owners (stockholders) receiving an adequate return on their investment?**

1. We want to know if the earnings available to the firm's owners or common equity investors are attractive when compared to the returns of owners of similar companies in the same industry.

2. Return on equity (ROE) $= \dfrac{\text{net income}}{\text{common equity}}$

3. The effect of using debt on net income: This example shows how, through the use of debt, firms can affect their return on equity.

4. Return on equity is a function of:

    (1) the operating return on assets less the interest rate paid, and

    (2) the amount of debt used in the capital structure relative to the equity.

E. **Question 5: Is the management team creating shareholder value?**

1. We want to know if management is creating or destroying shareholder value.

2. We use two approaches to answer this question.

    a. We examine the market-value ratios: Price/Earnings (PE) and Price/Book ratios.

    b. We estimate the value being created for shareholders using the Economic Value Added (EVA^{TM}).

IV. Limitations of Ratio Analysis

This list warns of the potential pitfalls that may be encountered in computing and interpreting financial ratios. Ratio users should be aware of these concerns prior to making decisions based solely on ratio analysis.

Study Problems

1.   Balance sheets for Marion Mfg. Co. and the Sterlington Corp. are found below. Both firms are involved in the manufacture of electrical components used in small electronic calculators and digital wristwatches. Since both firms are less than three years old, their book values are reasonably close to actual market value.

Marion Mfg. Co.
Balance Sheet
November 30, 2010

Assets		Liabilities & Equity	
Cash	$ 50,000	Notes payable	$ 520,000
Accounts receivable	90,000	(due in 30 days)	
Building	225,000	Accounts payable	420,000
Machinery	350,000	Owners' equity	150,000
Land	375,000		
	$1,090,000		$1,090,000

Sterlington Co.
Balance Sheet
November 30, 2010

Assets		Liabilities & Equity	
Cash	$ 50,000	Notes payable	$120,000
Accounts receivable	200,000	(due in 30 days)	
Land	10,000	Accounts payable	150,000
Machinery	350,000	Owners' equity	640,000
Building	300,000		
	$910,000		$910,000

(a)   Assume the role of a commercial banker who has been approached by both of the previous firms with a request for a 90-day loan for $200,000. For which of the firms are you most likely to approve the loan? Why?

(b)   If you were considering the purchase of one of these firms and assuming the liabilities of each, for which one would you be willing to pay the higher price? (Obviously, you would want more information in order to make a complete analysis, but make your evaluation based on the balance sheets above.)

SOLUTION

(a)   Sterlington Corp. In reviewing requests for short-term loans, the commercial loan officer is most interested in the liquidity of the subject firm. The current ratio of Marion Mfg. Co. is a very weak 0.15 while Sterlington Corp.'s current ratio is .93. In addition, a quick glance at the balance sheet of Marion Mfg. shows that a very substantial note of $520,000 comes due in 30 days, which the company may have difficulty paying.

(b)   Sterlington Corp. If it is assumed that book values are reasonably close to actual market values, the difference between Sterlington's total assets and assumed debt is $640,000, as opposed to Marion's net difference of $150,000.

2.   The financial manager of Sudhop, Inc. has just hired you (a recent finance graduate). Now he wishes to test your familiarity with financial ratios and your overall ability to work with financial statements. He gives you the following incomplete year-end balance sheet:

Sudhop, Inc.
Balance Sheet
December 31, 2010

Cash	$	Accounts payable	$
Accounts receivable		Long-term debt	
Inventory		Total Debt	$
Total current assets	$	Common stock	125,000
Fixed assets	400,000	Retained earnings	275,000
	$		$

He then gives you the following additional information and asks you to complete the above balance sheet.

Average collection period (assume a 360-day year)	30 days
Interest paid on long-term debt (10% rate)	$5,000
Debt-to-equity ratio	75%
Sales to total assets	2.0 times
Quick ratio	1.1
Current ratio	1.2

SOLUTION

Sudhop, Inc.
Balance Sheet
December 31, 2010

Cash	$225,000	Accounts payable	$250,000
Accounts receivable	50,000	Long-term debt	50,000
Inventory	25,000	Total Debt	$300,000
Total current assets	$300,000	Common stock	125,000
Fixed assets	400,000	Retained earnings	275,000
Total assets	$ 700,000	Total debt and equity	$700,000

Computations:

(a) Since debt to equity is 0.75, than debt must be $300,000 (0.75 x $400,000 equity).

(b) Debt plus equity equals total debt and equity and total assets, which comes to $700,000.

(c) Current assets equal total assets less fixed assets ($700,000 – $400,000).

(d) Since current assets ÷ current liabilities equals 1.20, then current liabilities equal $250,000 ($300,000 ÷ current liabilities = 1.2).

(e) Sales ÷ total assets = 2.0; so, sales ÷ $700 = 2.0; and sales = $1,400.

(f)   Accounts receivable may be determined to be $50,000 as follows:

$$\frac{\text{Average}}{\text{collection}} = \frac{\text{accounts receivable}}{\text{daily credit sales}}$$

From what we already know and assuming all sales are on credit,

$$30 = \frac{\text{accounts receivable}}{\$1,400 \div 360}.$$

(g)   Given a quick ratio of 1.1, inventory must be $25,000:

$$\frac{\$300,000 - \text{inventories}}{\$250,000} = 1.1.$$

(h)   Cash equals current assets minus accounts receivable and inventory.

3.   The balance sheet and income statement for Miller Company are given for the year 2010; various financial ratios for the industry in which Miller operates are also provided.

Miller Company
Balance Sheet
December 31, 2010
(000's)

Cash	$ 230	Notes payable	$ 1,015
Accounts receivable	9,380	Accounts payable	3,545
Inventories	7,515	Accrued taxes	225
Current assets	17,125	Current liabilities	4,785
Fixed assets (net)	34,125	Long-term debt	18,035
Total Assets	$51,250	Deferred income taxes	2,840
		Total Debt	$20,875
		Common stock-par	575
		Paid in capital	7,945
		Retained earnings	17,070
		Common equity	25,590
		Total liabilities	
		& net worth	$51,250

Miller Company
Income Statement
Year Ended December 31, 2010

Net sales (credit)	$46,235
Cost of sales	33,167
Gross profit	13,068
General and administrative expense	9,590
Operating income	3,478
Interest changes	1,120
Net income before taxes	2,358
Income taxes	1,130
Net income	$ 1,228

Industry Ratios

	Industry
Current ratio	4.02
Acid-test ratio	3.00
Inventory turnover	7.50
Average collection period	63.1
Operating profit margin	6.0%
Total asset turnover	2.0
Fixed asset turnover	3.0
Debt ratio	38.0%
Times interest earned	3.90
Return on equity	4.0%

Required:

Evaluate Miller's financial performance, using the "four-question approach" presented in Chapter 3 of the text.

SOLUTION

(a)

	Industry	Miller
Current ratio	4.02	3.58
Acid-test ratio	3.00	2.01
Inventory turnover	7.50	4.41
Average collection period	63.1	74.1
Operating profit margin	6.0%	7.5
Total asset turnover	2.0	0.9
Fixed asset turnover	3.0	1.4
Debt ratio	38.0%	50.1%
Times interest earned	3.90	3.11
Return on equity	4.0%	4.8%

(b) Miller's *liquidity* ratios are well below the industry averages. The most serious problem is with inventory turnover, which is almost half the industry norm.

The operating return on assets, OROA, for Miller and the industry are determined as follows:

Since OROA $=$ operating profit margin $\times$ total asset turnover

then:

Miller: 7.5% $\times$ 0.9 $=$ 6.8%

Industry: 6.0% $\times$ 2.0 $=$ 12%

Thus, Miller's management is not generating satisfactory operating profits on the firm's assets. However, Miller's operating profit margin exceeds the industry, which suggests that they are better than the average firm at some combination of the following.

1. receive above-average prices for their products.

2. sell more units of their products.

3. lower cost of goods sold.

4.   lower operating expenses (general and administrative and marketing).

However, the firm is clearly not using its assets efficiently to generate sales, as suggested by the turnover ratios and collection period.

The net effect of the operating profit margin and the asset turnovers is a low OROA.

The firm uses more debt to finance its assets, as reflected by the higher debt ratio and the lower times interest earned. The low times interest earned is also due to the lower OROA, which affects the numerator of the ratio.

Miller's stockholders received an above-average return on their investment (return on equity), but it was accomplished by using more debt, which exposes the investors to greater financial risk.

4.   Seward, Inc.'s, balance sheet shows a stockholders' book equity value of $300.000. The firm's earnings per share was $2, resulting in a price/earnings ratio of 8. There are 25,000 shares of common stock outstanding. What is the price/book ratio?

SOLUTION:

To calculate the price to book ratio, we need to determine the market price per share as well as the balance sheet book value per share. The market price is derived as follows:

$$\text{Earnings per share} = \frac{\text{Earnings}}{25,000 \text{ shares}} = \$2; \text{ Earnings} = \$50,000$$

$$\text{Price/Earnings} = \frac{\text{Price}}{\$2} = 8; \text{ Market price per share} = \mathbf{\$16}$$

$$\text{Book values per share} = \frac{\text{Equity Book Value}}{\text{Number of shares}} = \frac{\$300,000}{25,000 \text{ shares}} = \mathbf{\$12}$$

$$\frac{\text{Price}}{\text{Book}} = \frac{\$16}{\$12} = 1.33$$

During the past year, Winand, Inc. earned an operating income return on investment of 14 percent, compared to an industry norm of 10 percent. It has been estimated that the firm's investors have a required rate of return of 15 percent. The firm's total assets for the year were $400 million. Compute the amount of economic value created or destroyed by the firm.

SOLUTION

EVA = (14% – 15%) x $400 million = ($4 million)

Self-Tests

TRUE-FALSE

_____ 1. Accounts receivable turnover gives us the same information as the average collection period.

_____ 2. Operating return on assets is affected by the firm's operating profit margin and its debt ratio.

_____ 3. The operating profit margin is a measure of asset efficiency.

_____ 4. Return on equity is partly a function of operating return on assets.

_____ 5. Times interest earned is equal to net income divided by interest expense.

_____ 6. Operating return on assets is equal to operating profit margin times total asset turnover.

_____ 7. Operating profit margin measures how well management is managing the firm's income statement.

_____ 8. Liquidity is measured by the times interest earned ratio.

_____ 9. Total asset turnover tells us how efficiently management is using the firm's assets.

_____ 10. Financial ratios help us identify financial strengths and weaknesses of firms by way of being able to make meaningful comparisons of firm's financial data at different points in time and with other firms.

_____ 11. A firm's cash account is not considered in determining its liquidity.

_____ 12. The current ratio is more conservative than the acid-test ratio.

_____ 13. Inventory turnover and the average collection period may be used to measure the same thing—operating profitability.

_____ 14. Return on equity measures the dividends investors received in the current year.

_____ 15. The Economic Value Added (EVA^{TM}) is used to estimate a firm's liquidity and financing decisions.

MULTIPLE CHOICE

1. Which ratio does not help answer the question of adequate operating profitability generated by the firm's assets?

   a. operating return on assets
   b. return on common equity
   c. total asset turnover
   d. operating profit margin

2. Which ratio is used in both measuring a firm's liquidity and generating adequate operating profitability?

   a. average collection period
   b. operating profit margin
   c. acid-test ratio
   d. inventory turnover
   e. a and d

3. Which of the following is not used to evaluate how management is doing at creating shareholder value?

   a. Price/Earnings ratio
   b. Price/Book ratio
   c. operating profit margin
   d. Economic Value Added (EVA^{TM})

4. Current assets minus inventories over current liabilities is

   a. acid-test ratio.
   b. current ratio.
   c. average collection period.
   d. current asset turnover.

5. Return on Common equity is affected by which of the following?

   a. sales
   b. total asset turnover
   c. debt-equity ratio
   d. net profit margin
   e. all of the above

6.   What is the difference between the current ratio and the quick ratio?

    a.   inventories
    b.   Inventories is subtracted from the numerator.
    c.   Inventories is subtracted from the denominator.
    d.   The current ratio is more conservative.

7.   The ratio of total debt over total assets is

    a.   the current ratio.
    b.   the debt ratio.
    c.   a measure of a firm's liquidity.
    d.   referred to as the quick ratio because it is so easily determined.

8.   Robert Morris Associates and other published industry averages are

    a.   offered for every industry.
    b.   scientifically determined averages.
    c.   only approximations.
    d.   good for many years.

9.   An industry average is best used as

    a.   a desirable target or norm for the firm.
    b.   a guide to the financial position of the average firm in the industry.
    c.   a scientifically determined average of the ratios of a representative sample of firms within an industry.
    d.   a point or rule with which to measure profitability.

10.   Operating return on assets is affected by

    a.   depreciation expense.
    b.   interest expense.
    c.   income tax.
    d.   all of the above.

CHAPTER 5

The Time Value of Money

<u>Orientation</u>: In this chapter, the concept of a time value of money is introduced; that is, a dollar today is worth more than a dollar received a year from now. Thus, if we are to logically compare projects and financial strategies, we must move all dollar flows either back to the present or out to some common future date.

I. Compound interest results when the interest paid on the investment during the first period is added to the principal and during the second period the interest is earned on the original principal plus the interest earned during the first period.

    A. Mathematically, the future value of an investment if compounded annually at a rate of r for n years will be

$$FV_n = PV (1 + r)^n$$

        where n = the number of years during which the compounding occurs

             r = the annual interest (or discount) rate

          PV = the present value or original amount invested at the beginning of the first period

        FV_n = the future value of the investment at the end of n years

      1. The future value of an investment can be increased either by increasing the number of years we let it compound or by compounding it at a higher rate.

      2. If the compounded period is less than one year, the future value of an investment can be determined as follows:

$$FV_n = PV\left(1 + \frac{r}{m}\right)^{mn}$$

      where m = the number of times compounding occurs during the year

II. Determining the present value, that is, the value in today's dollars of a sum of money to be received in the future, involves nothing other than inverse, compounding. The differences in these techniques come about merely from the investor's point of view.

A. Mathematically, the present value of a sum of money to be received in the future can be determined with the following equation:

$$PV = FV_n \left(\frac{1}{(1 + r)^n} \right)$$

where n = the number of years until payment will be received,

r = the opportunity rate or discount rate,

PV = the present value of the future sum of money,

FV_n = the future value of the investment at the end of n years.

1. The present value of a future sum of money is inversely related to both the number of years until the payment will be received and the opportunity rate.

III. An annuity is a series of equal dollar payments for a specified number of years. Because annuities occur frequently in finance—for example, bond interest payments—we treat them specially.

A. A compound annuity involves depositing or investing an equal sum of money at the end of each year for a certain number of years and allowing it to grow.

1. This can be done by using our compounding equation and compounding each one of the individual deposits to the future or by using the following compound annuity equation:

$$FV_n = PMT \left(\sum_{t=0}^{n-1} (1 + r)^t \right) = PMT \left[\frac{(1+r)^n - 1}{r} \right]$$

where PMT = the annuity value deposited at the end of each year

r = the annual interest (or discount) rate

n = the number of years for which the annuity will last

FV_n = the future value of the annuity at the end of the nth year

B. Pension funds, insurance obligation, and interest received from bonds all involve annuities. To compare these financial instruments, we would like to know the present value of each of these annuities.

1. This can be done by using our present value equation and discounting each one of the individual cash flows back to the present or by using the following present value of an annuity equation:

$$PV = PMT\left(\sum_{t=1}^{n} \frac{1}{(1+r)^t}\right) = PMT\left[\frac{1 - \frac{1}{(1+r)^n}}{i}\right]$$

where PMT = the annuity withdrawn at the end of each year

r = the annual interest or discount rate

PV = the present value of the future annuity

n = the number of years for which the annuity will last

C. This procedure of solving for PMT, the annuity value when r, n, and PV are known, is also the procedure used to determine what payments are associated with paying off a loan in equal installments. Loans paid off in this way, in periodic payments, are called amortized loans. Here again, we know three of the four values in the annuity equation and are solving for a value of PMT, the annual annuity.

IV. A perpetuity is an annuity that continues forever; that is, this investment pays the same dollar amount every year from now on.

A. An example of a perpetuity is preferred stock that yields a constant dollar dividend infinitely.

B. The following equation can be used to determine the present value of a perpetuity:

$$PV = \frac{pp}{r}$$

where PV = the present value of the perpetuity

pp = the constant dollar amount provided by the perpetuity

r = the annual interest or discount rate

V. To aid in the calculations of present and future values, tables are provided at the back of the text.

A. To aid in determining the value of FV_n in the compounding formula

$$FV_n = PV(1+r)^n$$

The value of $(1+r)^n$ is referred to as FUTURE VALUE FACTOR$_{r,n}$ calculated as $(1+r)^n$.

B. To aid in the computation of present values

$$PV = FV_n \frac{1}{(1+r)^n}$$

With $\dfrac{1}{(1+r)^n}$, equal to the Present Value Factor

C. Because of the time-consuming nature of compounding an annuity,

$$FV_n = PMT \sum_{t=0}^{n-1}(1+r)^t \text{ where}$$

$$\sum_{t=0}^{n-1}(1+r)^t = \left[\frac{(1+r)^n - 1}{r}\right]$$

And is referred to as the ANNUITY PRESENT VALUE FACTOR$_{r,n}$

D. To simplify the process of determining the present value of an annuity

$$PV = PMT \left(\sum_{t=1}^{n}\frac{1}{(1+r)^t}\right) \text{ where}$$

$\sum_{t=1}^{n}\dfrac{1}{(1+r)^t}$ is referred to as the ANNUITY PRESENT VALUE

$$FACTOR_{r,n} = \left[\frac{1 - \dfrac{1}{(1+i)^n}}{i}\right]$$

Study Problems

1.   What will be the accumulated value of $1,000 invested for 10 years at 10% compounded annually?

SOLUTION

Substituting into the compound value formula, we get:

$$FV_n = PV(1 + i)^n$$

$$FV_{10} = \$1,000(1 + 0.10)^{10}$$

$$FV_{10} = \$1,000(2.594)$$

$$FV_{10} = \$2,594$$

Or:

N	=	10
I/Y	=	10
PV	=	-1,000
PMT	=	0
CPT FV =		**$2,594**

2.   How many years will it take $500 to grow to $1,586 if it is invested at 8% compounded annually?

SOLUTION

CPT N =		**15**
I/Y	=	8
PV	=	-500
PMT	=	0
FV	=	$1,586

3. At what annual rate would $1,000 have to be invested in order to grow to $4,046 in 10 years?

SOLUTION

$$N \quad = \quad 10$$

CPT I/Y = **15**

$$PV \quad = \quad -1,000$$

$$PMT \quad = \quad 0$$

$$FV \quad = \quad \$4,046$$

4. What is the present value of $1,000 to be received 8 years from now, discounted back to the present at 10%?

SOLUTION

$$N \quad = \quad 8$$

$$I/Y \quad = \quad 10$$

CPT PV = **467**

$$PMT \quad = \quad 0$$

$$FV \quad = \quad \$1,000$$

5. What is the accumulated sum of the following streams of payments: $1,000 per year for 5 years compounded annually at 5%?

SOLUTION

Substituting into the compound annuity formula, we get:

$$FV_n = PMT \sum_{t=0}^{n-1} (1+t)^t$$

$$FV_5 = \$1,000 \sum_{t=0}^{5-1} (1 + 0.05)^t$$

$$FV_5 = \$1,000(5.526)$$

$$FV_5 = \$5,526.$$

Or:

$$
\begin{aligned}
N &= 5 \\
I/Y &= 5 \\
PV &= 0 \\
PMT &= -1,000 \\
\textbf{CPT FV} &= \mathbf{\$5,526}
\end{aligned}
$$

6. What is the present value of $100 a year for 15 years discounted back to the present at 15%?

SOLUTION

Substituting into the present value of an annuity formula:

$$PV = PMT \left(\sum_{t=1}^{n} \frac{1}{(1+t)^t} \right)$$

$$PV = \$100 \left(\sum_{t=1}^{15} \frac{1}{(1+0.15)^t} \right)$$

$$PV = \$100(5.847)$$

$$PV = \$584.70.$$

Or:

$$
\begin{aligned}
N &= 15 \\
I/Y &= 15 \\
\textbf{CPT PV} &= \mathbf{584.74} \\
PMT &= -100 \\
FV &= 0
\end{aligned}
$$

7. If you receive a 9% $100,000 loan that has annual payments of $14,695.08, how many loan payments must you make in order to pay off the loan?

SOLUTION

CPT N =		**11**
I/Y	=	9
PV	=	-100,000
PMT	=	14,695.08
FV	=	0

8. At what annual rate would each of the following have to be invested?

(a) $550 to grow to $1,898.60 in 13 years

(b) $275 to grow to $406.18 in 8 years

(c) $60 to grow to $279.66 in 20 years

(d) $180 to grow to $486.00 in 6 years

SOLUTION

(a)

N	=	13
CPT I/Y =		**10**
PV	=	-550
PMT	=	0
FV	=	$1,898.60

(b)

N	=	8
CPT I/Y =		**5**
PV	=	-275
PMT	=	0
FV	=	$406.18

(c)

N	=	20
CPT I/Y =		**8**
PV	=	-60
PMT	=	0
FV	=	$279.66

(d)

N	=	6
CPT I/Y =		**18**
PV	=	-180
PMT	=	0
FV	=	$486

9.   What is the accumulated sum of each of the following streams of payments?

(a) $500 a year for 10 years compounded annually at 6%

(b) $150 a year for 5 years compounded annually at 11%

(c) $35 a year for 8 years compounded annually at 7%

(d) $25 a year for 3 years compounded annually at 2%

SOLUTION

(a) $$FV_n = PMT \left(\sum_{t=0}^{n-1} (1+i)^t \right)$$

$$FV_{10} = \$500 \left(\sum_{t=0}^{10-1} (1+0.06)^t \right)$$

$$FV_{10} = \$500\,(13.181)$$

$$FV_{10} = \$6,590.50$$

Or:

$$N = 10$$
$$I/Y = 6$$
$$PV = 0$$
$$PMT = -500$$

CPT FV = **$6,590.40**

(b) $FV_n = PMT \left(\sum_{t=0}^{n-1} (1+i)^t \right)$

$FV_5 = \$150 \left(\sum_{t=0}^{5-1} (1+0.11)^t \right)$

$FV_5 = \$150 \, (6.228)$

$FV_5 = \$934.20$

Or:

$$N = 5$$
$$I/Y = 11$$
$$PV = 0$$
$$PMT = -150$$

CPT FV = **$934**

(c) $FV_n = PMT \left(\sum_{t=0}^{n-1} (1+i)^t \right)$

$FV_7 = \$35 \left(\sum_{t=0}^{8-1} (1+0.07)^t \right)$

$FV_7 = \$35 \, (10.260)$

$FV_7 = \$359.10$

Or:

$$
\begin{array}{rcl}
N & = & 8 \\
I/Y & = & 7 \\
PV & = & 0 \\
PMT & = & -35 \\
\textbf{CPT FV} & = & \textbf{\$359}
\end{array}
$$

(d) $\quad FV_n \quad = \quad PMT \left(\displaystyle\sum_{t=0}^{n-1} (1+i)^t \right)$

$\qquad FV_3 \quad = \quad \$25 \left(\displaystyle\sum_{t=0}^{3-1} (1+0.02)^t \right)$

$\qquad FV_3 \quad = \quad \$25\,(3.060)$

$\qquad FV_3 \quad = \quad \$76.50$

Or:

$$
\begin{array}{rcl}
N & = & 3 \\
I/Y & = & 2 \\
PV & = & 0 \\
PMT & = & -25 \\
\textbf{CPT FV} & = & \textbf{\$76.51}
\end{array}
$$

10.   Hanna purchased a new house for $150,000. She paid $30,000 down and agreed to pay the rest over the next 25 years in 25 equal annual payments that include principal payments plus 10% compound interest on the unpaid balance. What will these equal payments be?

SOLUTION

$$
\begin{array}{rcl}
N & = & 25 \\
I/Y & = & 10 \\
PV & = & -120,000 \\
\textbf{CPT PMT} & = & \textbf{13,220} \\
FV & = & 0
\end{array}
$$

11. How much do you have to deposit today so that beginning 11 years from now you can withdraw $10,000 a year for the next five years (periods 11 through 15) plus an *additional* amount of $15,000 in that last year (period 15)? Assume an interest rate of 7%.

SOLUTION

Step 1: First, discount the annuity back to the beginning of year 11, which is the end of year 10. Then, discount this equivalent sum to present.

$$PV = PMT\left(\sum_{t=1}^{n} \frac{1}{(1+i)^t}\right)$$

$$= \$10,000\left(\sum_{t=1}^{5} \frac{1}{(1+.07)^t}\right)$$

$$= \$10,000(4.100)$$

$$= \$41,000 \text{ — then discount the equivalent sum}$$

back to present.

Step 2: Then discount the $41,000 back to present (it is now at the end of year 10).

$$PV = FV_n\left(\frac{1}{(1+i)^n}\right)$$

$$PV = \$41,000\left(\frac{1}{(1+.07)^{10}}\right)$$

$$PV = \$41,000(.508)$$

$$PV = \$20,828$$

Then add the present value of the $15,000 withdrawal at the end of year 15 to this amount.

$$PV = FV_{15}\left(\frac{1}{(1+.07)^{15}}\right)$$

$$= \$15,000(.362)$$

$$= \$5,430$$

Thus, you would have to deposit $20,828 + $5,430 or $26,258 today.

Or:

Step 1 (First, discount the annuity back to the beginning of year 11, which is the end of year 10.).

N	=	5
I/Y	=	7
CPT PV	=	**-41,002**
PMT	=	10,000
FV	=	0

Step 2 (Then, discount this equivalent sum to the present.).

N	=	10
I/Y	=	7
CPT PV	=	**23,473**
PMT	=	0
FV	=	-20,843

Step 3 (Then, determine the present value of the $15,000 withdrawal at the end of year 15).

N	=	15
I/Y	=	7
CPT PV	=	**5,437**
PMT	=	0
FV	=	-15,000

Step 4: (Add the present values together):

Thus, you would have to deposit $20,843 + $5,437 or $26,280 today.

Self Tests

TRUE-FALSE

_____ 1. The fact that there is an opportunity cost to money brings on the concept of the time value of money.

_____ 2. The higher the rate used to compound a given sum, the larger it will be at some future date.

_____ 3. The future value of an investment can be increased by reducing the number of years we let it compound.

_____ 4. There is an inverse relationship between the present value of a future cash flow and the discount rate.

_____ 5. Daily, as opposed to annual, compounding takes on importance because it allows interest to be earned on interest more frequently.

_____ 6. Determining present value is merely the inverse of compounding.

_____ 7. A compound annuity involves depositing or investing an equal sum of money at the end of each year for a certain number of years and allowing it to grow.

_____ 8. A perpetuity is an annuity that continues for 30 years or more.

_____ 9. The present value of an annuity increases as the discount rate decreases.

_____ 10. An example of perpetuity is the interest received on long-term bonds.

MULTIPLE CHOICE

1.   To determine the present value of a future sum, we need only multiply it by

   a. $\dfrac{1}{(1+i)^n}$.

   b. $\dfrac{1}{(1+n)^i}$.

   c. $(1 + n)^i$.
   d. $(1 + i)^n$.

2.   The present value of a $100 perpetuity discounted back to the present at 6% is

   a. $6,000.00.
   b. $6,666.66.
   c. $1,666.67.
   d. $1,200.00.

3.   If we place $100 in a savings account that yields 6% compounded semiannually, what will our investment grow to at the end of five years?

   a. $133.80
   b. $130.00
   c. $125.00
   d. $134.40

4.   A bond maturing in 10 years pays $80 each year and $1,000 upon maturity. Assuming 10% to be the appropriate discount rate, the present value of the bond is

   a. $1,010.84.
   b. $925.74.
   c. $877.60.
   d. $1,000.00.

5.   The Fuller Company has received a $50,000 loan. The annual payments are $6,202.70. If the Fuller Company is paying 9% interest per year, how many loan payments must the company make?

   a.   15
   b.   13
   c.   12
   d.   19

CHAPTER 6

The Meaning and Measurement of Risk and Return

Orientation: In this chapter, we examine the factors that determine rates of return (discount rates) in the capital markets. We are particularly interested in the relationship between risk and rates of return. We look at risk both in terms of the riskiness of an individual security and that of a portfolio of securities.

I.   Expected Return Defined and Measured

    A.   The expected benefits or returns to be received from an investment come in the form of the cash flows the investment generates.

    B.   The rate of return earned from an investment can be calculated as the ratio of the dollar gain divided by the amount of the investment at the beginning of the period. We can formalize these calculations as follows:

Holding-period *dollar gain*

$$\text{Holding-period dollar gain, DG} = \text{Price}_{\substack{\text{end of} \\ \text{period}}, P_{\text{end}}} + \text{cash distribution (dividend,Div)} - \text{Price}_{\substack{\text{beginning} \\ \text{of period}}, P_{\text{begin}}}$$

$$= \frac{\text{Price}_{\text{end of period}} - \text{Price}_{\text{beginning of period}}}{\text{Price}_{\text{beginning of period}}}$$

and for the holding–period *rate of return*

$$\text{Rate of return, } r = \frac{\text{dollar gain}}{P_{\text{begin}}} = \frac{P_{\text{end}} + Div - P_{\text{begin}}}{P_{\text{begin}}}$$

C. In an uncertain world, we must use expected cash flows, $\bar{X}$, for computing expected gains and rates of return. We compute an expected cash flow as follows:

$$\bar{X} \quad = \quad P(X_1)X_1 + P(X_2)X_2 + \cdots + P(X_n)X_n$$

where n = the number of possible states of the economy
X_i = the cash flow in the *ith* state of the economy
$P(X_i)$ = the probability of the *ith* cash flow

II. Risk Defined and Measured

A. Risk can be defined as the possible variation in cash flow in an expected cash flow.

B. Statistically, risk may be measured by the standard deviation in the expected cash flow.

III. Rates of Return: The Investors' Experience

A. Data have been compiled by Ibbotson and Associates on the actual returns for various portfolios of securities from 1926-1998.

B. The following portfolios were studied:

1. Common stocks of large firms
2. Common stocks of small firms
3. Corporate bonds
4. Long-term U.S. government bonds
5. Intermediate U.S. government bonds
6. U.S. Treasury bills

C. Investors historically have received greater returns for greater risk taking with the exception of long-term U.S. government bonds.

D. The only portfolio with returns consistently exceeding the inflation rate has been common stocks.

IV. Risk and Diversification

A. The market rewards diversification. We can lower risk without sacrificing expected return, and/or we can increase expected return without having to assume more risk.

B. Diversifying among different kinds of assets is called asset allocation. Compared to diversification within the different asset classes, the benefits received are far greater through effective asset allocation.

C.   Total variability can be divided into:

    1.   The variability of returns unique to the security (diversifiable or unsystematic risk)

    2.   The risk related to market movements (nondiversifiable or systematic risk)

D.   By diversifying, the investor can eliminate the "unique" security risk. The systematic risk, however, cannot be diversified away.

E.   Measuring Market Risk

    1.   The **characteristic line** tells us the average movement in a firm's stock price in response to a movement in the general market, such as the S&P 500 Index. The slope of the characteristic line, which has come to be called **beta**, is a measure of a stock's systematic or market risk. The slope of the line is merely the ratio of the "rise" of the line relative to the "run" of the line.

    2.   If a security's beta equals one, a 10 percent increase (decrease) in market returns will produce on average a 10 percent increase (decrease) in security returns.

    3.   A security having a higher beta is more volatile and thus more risky than a security having a lower beta value.

F.   A portfolio's beta is equal to the average of the betas of the stocks in the portfolio.

G.   Risk and diversification can be demonstrated by a comparison of three portfolios consisting of short-term government securities, long-term government bonds, and large-company stocks.

V.   The Investor's Required Rate of Return

A.   The required rate of return is the minimum rate necessary to compensate an investor for accepting the risk he or she associates with the purchase and ownership of an asset.

B.   Two factors determine the required rate of return for the investor:

    1.   The risk-free rate of interest, which recognizes the time value of money.

    2.   The risk premium, which considers the riskiness (variability of returns) of the asset and the investor's attitude toward risk.

C.   Capital asset pricing model—CAPM

   1.   The required rate of return for a given security can be expressed as

$$\begin{array}{c}\text{Required} \\ \text{rate}\end{array} = \begin{array}{c}\text{risk-free} \\ \text{rate}\end{array} + \text{beta} \times \left(\begin{array}{cc}\text{market} & \text{risk-free} \\ \text{return} & \text{rate}\end{array}\right)$$

   or

$$k_j = k_{rf} + \beta_j \,(k_m - k_{rf})$$

   2.   Security market line

      a.   Graphically illustrates the CAPM.

      b.   Designates the risk-return trade-off existing in the market, where risk is defined in terms of beta according to the CAPM equation.

Study Problems

   1.   Phillips, Inc. is considering an investment in one of two common stocks. Given the information below, which investment is better, based on risk and return?

Common Stock A		Common Stock B	
Probability	*Return*	*Probability*	*Return*
0.10	–10%	0.30	5%
0.20	6	0.20	12
0.40	15	0.40	10
0.30	9	0.10	20

SOLUTION

   Common Stock A

      Expected Return

$$= 0.1(-10\%) + 0.2(6\%) + 0.4(15\%) + 0.3(9\%)$$
$$= -1\% + 1.2\% + 6\% + 2.7\% = 8.9\%$$

Standard Deviation

$$= [(-10\% - 8.9\%)^2(0.10) + (6\% - 8.9\%)^2(0.2)$$
$$+ (15\% - 8.9\%)^2 (0.4) + (9\% - 8.9\%)^2(0.30)]^{1/2}$$
$$= (35.721\% + 1.682\% + 14.884\% + 0.003\%)^{1/2} = .23\%$$

Common Stock B

Expected Return

$$= 0.3(5\%) + 0.2(12\%) + 0.4(10\%) + 0.10(20\%)$$
$$= 1.5\% + 2.4\% + 4\% + 2\% = 9.9\%$$

Standard Deviation

$$= [(5\% - 9.9\%)^2(0.3) + (12\% - 9.9\%)^2(0.2)$$
$$+ (10\% - 9.9\%)^2(0.4) + (20\% - 9.9\%)^2(0.1)]^{1/2}$$
$$= (7.203\% + 0.882\% + 0.004\% + 10.201\%)^{1/2} = 4.28\%$$

Common stock B has both a higher expected return and a smaller standard deviation (less risk). Hence, B is better.

2.   Compute the annual holding-period return for the following stock.

Year	Stock Price
2007	$98
2008	105
2009	115
2010	100
2011	120

SOLUTION

Year	Return
2007	
2008	7.1%
2009	9.5%
2010	−13.0%
2011	20.0%

3. From the graph below, estimate Archie's beta.

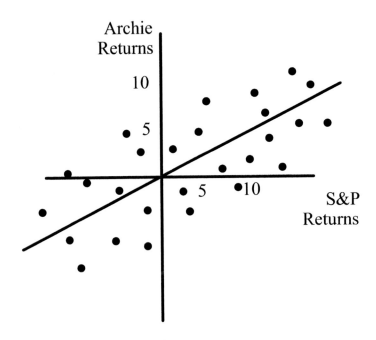

SOLUTION

Archie's beta is about 0.50. Archie's returns change about 5% while the market's returns change 10%, thus, 5 ÷ 10 = 0.50.

4. BC, Incorporated, has a beta of 0.65. If the expected market return is 10% and the risk-free rate is 5%, what is the appropriate expected return of BC, Incorporated?

SOLUTION

Expected return of BC, Incorporated

$$= \text{risk-free rate} + \text{Beta} \begin{pmatrix} \text{expected} & \text{risk} \\ \text{market} & - & \text{free} \\ \text{return} & \text{rate} \end{pmatrix}$$

$$= 5\% + 0.65(10\% - 5\%)$$

$$= 5\% + 3.25\% = 8.25\%$$

Self Tests

TRUE-FALSE

_____ 1. The investor's required rate of return is the minimum rate necessary to attract an investor to purchase or hold a security.

_____ 2. Risk, as defined in this chapter, is the variation in returns in an expected value.

_____ 3. Time value of money can be represented by a risk-free rate of return only for risk-free securities.

_____ 4. A proxy for the risk-free rate is the Corporate AA Bond rate.

_____ 5. An investor's required rate of return is always greater than the expected rate of return.

_____ 6. By proper diversification, an investor can eliminate the market-related (systematic) risk.

_____ 7. A security having a beta of one will move up (or down) on average with the market by the same percentage.

_____ 8. The addition of a security with a beta of zero provides no additional risk to a well-diversified portfolio.

_____ 9. The annual return on common stock historically has been greater than that of U.S. Treasury bills.

_____ 10. A security with an expected return of 15.9% and a standard deviation of 9.8% is obviously better than a Treasury bill earning 8%.

_____ 11. The real average annual rate of return is the nominal return minus the risk-free rate of return.

_____ 12. Corporate bonds are always more risky than Treasury bills and long-term government bonds.

MULTIPLE CHOICE

1. Under the capital-asset pricing model, the relevant risk is

    a. diversifiable risk.
    b. systematic risk.
    c. financial risk.
    d. standard deviation.

2. If the required return for a security is 15% and the risk-free rate is 6%, the risk premium is

    a. 0%.
    b. 6%.
    c. 10%.
    d. 9%.
    e. 15%.

3. In terms of the security market line, a security with a beta of 1.5 should provide a risk premium _____ times the risk premium existing for the market as a whole.

    a. 0
    b. 1
    c. 1.5
    d. 2.5
    e. 0.5

4. The beta for a portfolio is determined by

    a. calculating the standard deviation of the betas of the individual stocks in the portfolio.
    b. computing the unweighted average of the individual betas.
    c. calculating a weighted average of the individual stock betas, where the weights equal the individual stocks' expected returns.
    d. calculating a weighted average of the individual stock betas, where the weights equal the percentage invested in each stock.

5.   A stock's holding period return represents

    a.   the dividend received each period.
    b.   the rate of return that would be earned on a stock if bought at the beginning of the period and sold at the end of the period.
    c.   the return received from diversifying one's portfolio.
    d.   the return from a stock relative to the return of the portfolio.

6.   An investor's required rate of return should be a function of

    a.   the riskiness of the investment being made without regard for the riskiness of other investments.
    b.   the risk-free rate of return less the inflation rate.
    c.   the risk-free rate of return plus the inflation rate.
    d.   the risk-free rate of return plus a risk premium for the stock's systematic risk.

7.   You should expect a higher rate of return from

    a.   long-term corporate bonds than from common stocks.
    b.   small company stocks than from common stocks of large firms.
    c.   U.S. Treasury bills than from long-term government securities.
    d.   none of the above.

8.   Market risk can also be called

    a.   unsystematic risk.
    b.   non-diversifiable risk.
    c.   diversifiable risk.
    d.   firm-specific risk.
    e.   company-unique risk.

9.   _____ is the only risk that matters to investors with broadly diversified portfolios.

    a.   Systematic risk
    b.   Unsystematic risk
    c.   Firm-specific risk
    d.   Diversifiable risk

CHAPTER 7

The Valuation and Characteristics of Bonds

Orientation: This chapter introduces the concepts that underlie asset valuation. We are specifically concerned with bonds. We also look at the concept of the bondholder's expected rate of return on an investment.

I.   Types of bonds

    A.   **Debentures:** unsecured long-term debt.

    B.   **Subordinated debentures:** bonds that have a lower claim on assets in the event of liquidation than do other senior debt holders.

    C.   **Mortgage bonds:** bonds secured by a lien on specific assets of the firm, such as real estate.

    D.   **Eurobonds:** bonds issued in a country different from the one in whose currency the bond is denominated; for instance, a bond issued in Europe or Asia that pays interest and principal in U.S. dollars.

    E.   **Convertible bonds:** Bonds that can be converted into common stock at a pre-specified price per share.

II.   Terminology and characteristics of bonds

    A.   A bond is a long-term promissory note that promises to pay the bondholder a predetermined, fixed amount of interest each year until maturity. At maturity, the principal will be paid to the bondholder.

    B.   In the case of a firm's insolvency, a bondholder has a priority of claim to the firm's assets before the preferred and common stockholders. Also, bondholders must be paid interest due them before dividends can be distributed to the stockholders.

    C.   A bond's par value is the amount that will be repaid by the firm when the bond matures, usually $1,000.

D. The contractual agreement of the bond specifies a **coupon interest rate** that is expressed either as a percent of the par value or as a flat amount of interest which the borrowing firm promises to pay the bondholder each year. For example: A $1,000 par value bond specifying a coupon interest rate of nine percent is equivalent to an annual interest payment of $90.

   1. When the investor receives a fixed interest rate, the bonds are called **fixed-rate bonds.**

   2. Sometimes a company will issue bonds at a substantial discount from their $1,000 face value with a zero or very low coupon, thus the name **zero-coupon bonds.**

E. The bond has a **maturity date,** at which time the borrowing firm is committed to repay the loan principal.

F. A convertible bond allows the investor to exchange the bond for a predetermined number of the firm's shares of common stock.

G. A bond is **callable or redeemable** when it provides the firm with the right to pay off the bond at some time before its maturity date. These bonds frequently have a **call protection period** which prevents the firm from calling the bond for a pre-specified time period.

H. An indenture (or trust deed) is the legal agreement between the firm issuing the bonds and the bond trustee who represents the bondholders. It provides the specific terms of the bond agreement such as the rights and responsibilities of both parties.

I. Bond ratings

   1. Bond ratings are simply judgments about the future risk potential of the bond in question. Bond ratings are extremely important in that a firm's bond rating tells much about the cost of funds and the firm's access to the debt market.

   2. Three primary rating agencies exist—Moody's, Standard & Poor's, and Fitch Investor Services.

   3. A **junk bond** is high-risk debt with *ratings of BB or below* by Moody's and Standard & Poor's. The lower the rating, the higher the chance of default

III. Definitions of value

A. Book value is the value of an asset shown on a firm's balance sheet which is determined by its historical cost rather than its current worth.

B.   Liquidation value is the amount that could be realized if an asset is sold individually and not as part of a going concern.

C.   Market value is the observed value of an asset in the marketplace where buyers and sellers negotiate an acceptable price for the asset.

D.   Intrinsic value is the value based upon the expected cash flows from the investment, the riskiness of the asset, and the investor's required rate of return. It is the value in the eyes of the investor and is the same as the present value of expected future cash flows to be received from the investment.

IV.   Valuation: An Overview

    A.   Value is a function of three elements:

        1.   The amount and timing of the asset's expected cash flow

        2.   The riskiness of these cash flows

        3.   The investors' required rate of return for undertaking the investment

    B.   Expected cash flows are used in measuring the returns from an investment.

V.   Valuation: The Basic Process

The value of an asset is found by computing the present value of all the future cash flows expected to be received from the asset. Expressed as a general present value equation, the value of an asset is found as follows:

$$V = \frac{\$C_1}{(1+r)^1} + \frac{\$C_2}{(1+r)^2} + \cdots + \frac{\$C_n}{(1+r)^n}$$

where C_t = the cash flow to be received at time t

V = the intrinsic value or present value of an asset producing expected future cash flows, C_{t}, in years 1 through N

r = the investor's required rate of return

n = the number of periods

VI. Bond Valuation

A. The value of a bond is simply the present value of the future interest payments and maturity value discounted at the bondholder's required rate of return. This may be expressed as:

$$V_b = \frac{\$I_1}{(1+r_b)^1} + \frac{\$I_2}{(1+r_b)^2} + \cdots + \frac{\$I_n}{(1+r_b)^n} + \frac{\$M}{(1+r_b)^n}$$

where I_t = the dollar interest to be received in each payment

M = the par value of the bond at maturity

r_b = the required rate of return for the bondholder

n = the number of periods to maturity

In other words, we are discounting the expected future cash flows to the present at the appropriate discount rate (required rate of return).

B. If interest payments are received semiannually (as with most bonds) the valuation equation becomes:

$$V_b = \frac{\$I_1/2}{\left(1+\dfrac{r_b}{2}\right)^1} + \frac{\$I_2/2}{\left(1+\dfrac{r_b}{2}\right)^2} + \cdots + \frac{\$I_{2n}/2}{\left(1+\dfrac{r_b}{2}\right)^{2n}} + \frac{\$M}{\left(1+\dfrac{r_b}{2}\right)^{2n}}$$

VII. Bond Yields

A. Yield to maturity

1. The yield to maturity is the rate of return the investor will earn if the bond is held to maturity, provided that the company issuing the bond does not default on the payments.

2 We compute the yield to maturity by finding the discount rate that gets the present value of the future interest payments and principal payment just equal to the bond's current market price.

B. Current yield

1. The current yield on a bond is the ratio of the annual interest payment o the bond's current market price.

2 The current yield is not an accurate measure of the bondholder's expected rate of return from holding the bond to maturity.

VIII. Bond Value: Three Important Relationships

  A. First relationship

    A decrease in interest rates (required rates of return) will cause the value of a bond to increase; an interest rate increase will cause a decrease in value. The change in value caused by changing interest rates is called **interest rate risk.**

  B. Second relationship

    1. If the bondholder's required rate of return (current interest rate) equals the coupon interest rate, the bond will sell at par, or maturity value.

    2. If the current interest rate exceeds the bond's coupon rate, the bond will sell below par value or at a "discount."

    3. If the current interest rate is less than the bond's coupon rate, the bond will sell above par value or at a "premium."

  C. Third relationship

    A bondholder owning a long-term bond is exposed to greater interest rate risk than when owning a short-term bond.

Study Problems

1. Gents Clothiers, Inc. has bonds maturing in 6 years and pays 6% interest semiannually on a $1000 face value.

    a. If your required rate of return is 10%, what is the value of the bond?

    b. How would your answer change if the interest were paid annually?

SOLUTION

a. Value of bond if interest is paid semiannually:

$$\text{Value } (V_b) = \sum_{t=1}^{12} \frac{\$30}{(1 + .05)^{12}} + \frac{\$1,000}{(1 + .05)^{12}}$$

$$= \$822.73$$

12	N			
5	I/Y			
30	PMT			
1000	FV			
CPT	PV	→	ANSWER	-822.73

b. Value of bond if interest is paid annually:

$$\text{Value } (V_b) = \sum_{t=1}^{6} \frac{\$60}{(1 + .10)^{6}} + \frac{\$1,000}{(1 + .10)^{16}}$$

$$= \$825.79$$

6	N			
10	I/Y			
60	PMT			
1000	FV			
CPT	PV	→	ANSWER	-825.79

2.   Edge Manufacturing Corporation's bonds are selling in the market for $1,193.96. These 15-year bonds pay 8% interest (annually) on a $1,000 par value. If they are purchased at the market price, what is the expected rate of return?

SOLUTION

$$\$1193.96 \quad = \sum_{t=1}^{15} \frac{\$80}{(1 + \overline{r}_b)^t} \quad + \quad \frac{\$1,000}{(1 + \overline{r}_b)^{15}}$$

15	$\boxed{N}$		
1193.96	$\boxed{PV}$		
80	$\boxed{PMT}$		
1000	$\boxed{FV}$		
$\boxed{CPT}$	$\boxed{I/Y} \rightarrow$	ANSWER	6%

3.   The market price is $865.60 for a 5-year, 12% bond ($1,000 face value) that pays interest semiannually. What is the expected rate of return?

SOLUTION

$$\$865.60 \quad = \sum_{t=1}^{10} \frac{\$60}{(1 + \overline{r}_b)^t} \quad + \quad \frac{\$1,000}{(1 + \overline{r}_b)^{10}}$$

10	$\boxed{N}$		
865.60	$\boxed{PV}$		
60	$\boxed{PMT}$		
1000	$\boxed{FV}$		
$\boxed{CPT}$	$\boxed{I/Y} \rightarrow$	ANSWER	8% semiannually
			16% annually

Self Tests

TRUE-FALSE

_____ 1. The par value of a bond is essentially independent of the market value of a bond.

_____ 2. The only variable that can cause the value of a bond to increase or decrease is a change in the bondholder's required rate of return.

_____ 3. In an efficient marketplace, the intrinsic value of a security will equal its market value.

_____ 4. If the market price of a security is larger than the value assigned to the security by an investor, then the expected rate is greater than the required rate of return.

_____ 5. Bond ratings indicate the chance that the bondholder will experience interest rate risk with a given bond.

_____ 6. The intrinsic value of an asset can be defined as the present value of the asset's expected future cash flows.

_____ 7. The yield to maturity of a bond is the current value of the bond.

_____ 8. The three items that directly affect the cash flows from owning a bond are the bond's par value, maturity date, and the coupon rate of interest.

_____ 9. The expected rate of return is equal to the required rate of return of bondholders who are willing to pay the present market price for the bonds.

_____ 10. An increase in interest rates will cause the value of a bond to increase.

_____ 11. An increase in interest automatically drives bonds' stated rates up.

_____ 12. Changes in interest rates have a greater impact on the value of short-term bonds as opposed to the value of long-term bonds.

_____ 13. The stated coupon rate of interest has no effect on the market price of a bond.

_____ 14. Investors are attracted to zero-coupon bonds by their high periodic interest payments.

_____ 15. In the case of insolvency, bondholders are honored before common stock but after preferred stock.

_____ 16. A bond denominated by yen, issued in Japan, and not registered with the SEC, could not be classified as a Eurobond.

_____ 17. Junk bonds differ from high-yield bonds in that junk bonds will almost always carry a lower rating than high-yield bonds.

_____ 18. In an efficient marketplace, the intrinsic value of a security will equal its market value.

MULTIPLE CHOICE

1. For a $1,000 par-value bond carrying an 8% coupon (interest paid quarterly) and having a 10% yield to maturity, the quarterly interest payments would be

   a. $20.
   b. $30.
   c. $25.
   d. $50.
   e. $10.

2. The value of a security may be expressed as a function of

   a. expected cash flows.
   b. riskiness of cash flows.
   c. the investor's required rate of return.
   d. a and b only.
   e. a, b, and c.

3. If the market is in equilibrium, the expected rate of return and the required rate of return

   a. will be the same.
   b. will be different.
   c. have no relationship to each other.

4.   If everything else is assumed to be constant, as the investor's required rate of return decreases, the value of a security

   a.   stays the same.
   b.   increases.
   c.   decreases.
   d.   has no relationship to the investor's required rate of return.

5.   In the basic security valuation model

$$V = \frac{\$C_1}{(1+r)^1} + \frac{\$C_2}{(1+r)^2} + \cdots + \frac{\$C_n}{(1+r)^n},$$

   C_1 stands for

   a.   the investor's required rate of return.
   b.   cash flow to be received in year 1.
   c.   the intrinsic value of an asset producing expected future cash flows.
   d.   none of the above.

6.   The _____ of an asset is the observed value for the asset in the marketplace.

   a.   intrinsic value
   b.   liquidation value
   c.   market value
   d.   None of the above are true.

7.   The _____ is the legal agreement that provides the specific terms of the loan agreement.

   a.   mortgage
   b.   debenture
   c.   indenture
   d.   prospectus

8.   A(n) _____ is a bond secured by a lien on real property.

a.   mortgage bond
b.   subordinated debenture
c.   Eurobond
d.   coupon bond

9.   Junk bonds have all except which of the following characteristics?

a.   rated BB or lower
b.   low rates of return
c.   highly speculative
d.   no security

10.   Bond valuation depends on all but

a.   the amount of cash flows to be received.
b.   the maturity date of the loan.
c.   the investor's required rate of return.
d.   when the loan was issued.

11.   When a bond is worth more than its face value, it is said to sell

a.   at a discount.
b.   at a premium.
c.   at its maturity value.
d.   above its market return.

12.   When the market interest rate rises above the stated interest rate of a bond, the bond

a.   will sell at a discount.
b.   will sell at a premium.
c.   will sell at its par or stated value.
d.   will not sell because investors can receive a better return from the market.

13.   The risk of changing bond values due to the variability of future interest rates is

a.   time value of money.
b.   interest-rate risk.
c.   timing risk.
d.   investment risk.

14. The current yield on a bond refers to

   a. the interest payments due within the next year.
   b. the ratio of the annual interest payment to the bond's market price.
   c. the interest earned in the current period.
   d. the coupon rate of interest.

15. Bond ratings are affected favorably by all except which of the following?

   a. profitable operations
   b. large firm size
   c. low variability in past earnings
   d. taking more advantage of financial leverage

16. When bond prices are quoted, they are generally expressed at

   a. par value.
   b. face value.
   c. a percentage of par value.
   d. current yield.

17. The current interest rate can also be called

   a. the yield to maturity.
   b. the coupon interest rate.
   c. the expected rate of return.
   d. the risk premium.
   e. a and c.

CHAPTER 8

The Valuation and Characteristics of Stock

Orientation: This chapter continues the introduction begun in Chapter 7 of the concepts underlying asset valuation. We are specifically concerned with valuing preferred stock and common stock. We also look at the concept of a stockholder's expected rate of return on an investment.

I.   Preferred Stock

    A.   Features of preferred stock

        1.   Owners of preferred stock receive dividends instead of interest.

        2.   Most preferred stocks are perpetuities (non-maturing).

        3.   Multiple classes, each having different characteristics, can be issued.

        4.   In the case of bankruptcy, preferred stock has priority over common stock with regard to claims on assets.

        5.   Most preferred stock carries a cumulative feature that requires all past unpaid preferred stock dividends to be paid before any common stock dividends are declared.

        6.   Preferred stock may contain other protective provisions.

        7.   Preferred stock contains provisions to convert to a predetermined number of shares of common stock.

        8.   Retirement features for preferred stock are frequently included.

            a.   Callable preferred refers to a feature which allows preferred stock to be called or retired, like a bond.

            b.   A sinking fund provision requires the firm to periodically set aside an amount of money for the retirement of its preferred stock.

B. Valuation of preferred stock (Vps):

The value of a preferred stock equals the present value of all future dividends. If the stock is nonmaturing, where dividends are expected in equal amount each year in perpetuity, the value may be calculated as follows:

$$V_{ps} = \frac{\text{annual dividend}}{\text{required rate of return}} =$$

II. Common Stock

A. Features of Common Stock

1. As owners of the corporation, common shareholders have the right to residual income and assets after bondholders and preferred stockholders have been paid.

2. Common stock shareholders are generally the only security holders with the right to elect the board of directors.

3. Preemptive rights entitle the common shareholder to maintain a proportionate share of ownership in the firm.

4. Common stock shareholders' liability as owners of the corporation is limited to the amount of their investment.

5. Common stock's value is equal to the present value of all future cash flows expected to be received by the stockholder.

B. Valuing common stock using the dividend valuation model

1. Company growth occurs either by:

a. The infusion of new capital.

b. The retention of earnings, which we call internal growth. The internal growth rate of a firm equals:

$$\text{Return on equity} \times \left(\begin{array}{l} \text{Percentage of earnings} \\ \text{retained within the firm} \end{array} \right)$$

2. Although the bondholder and preferred stockholder are promised a specific amount each year, the dividend for common stock is based on the profitability of the firm and the management's decision either to pay dividends or retain profits for reinvestment.

3. The common dividend typically increases along with growth in corporate earnings.

4. The earnings growth of a firm should be reflected in a higher price for the firm's stock.

5.   In finding the value of a common stock (V_{cs}), we should discount all future expected dividends (D_1, D_2, D_3, D_∞) to the present at the required rate of return for the stockholder (r_{cs}). That is:

$$V_{cs} = \frac{D_1}{(1+r_{cs})^1} + \frac{D_2}{(1+r_{cs})^2} + ... + \frac{D_\infty}{(1+r_{cs})^\infty}$$

6.   If we assume that the amount of dividend is increasing by a constant growth rate each year; that is, the dividend in year t, D_t, equals:

$$D_t = D_0 (1+g)^t$$

where g = the growth rate

D_0 = the most recent dividend payment

If the growth rate, g, is the same each year and is less than the required rate of return, r_{cs}, the valuation equation for common stock can be reduced to

$$V_{cs} = \frac{D_1}{r_{cs}-g} = \frac{D_0(1+g)}{r_{cs}-g}$$

III.   Shareholder's Expected Rate of Return

A.   The shareholder's expected rate of return is of great interest to financial mangers because it tells about the investor's expectations.

B.   Preferred stockholder's expected rate of return.

If we know the market price of a preferred stock and the amount of the dividends to be received, the expected rate of return from the investment can be determined as follows:

$$\text{expected rate of return} = \frac{\text{annual dividend}}{\text{market price of the stock}}$$

or

$$\bar{r}_{ps} = \frac{D}{P_{ps}}$$

C.   Common stockholder's expected rate of return

1.   The expected rate of return for common stock can be calculated from the valuation equations discussed earlier.

2.   Assuming that dividends are increasing at a constant annual growth rate (g), we can show that the expected rate of return for common stock, $\bar{r}_{cs}$ is

$$\bar{r}_{cs} \quad = \quad \left(\frac{\text{dividend in year 1}}{\text{market price}}\right) \;+\; \left(\begin{array}{c}\text{growth} \\ \text{rate}\end{array}\right)$$

$$= \quad \frac{D_1}{P_{cs}} \;+\; g$$

Since dividend ÷ price is the "dividend yield," the

$$\text{Expected rate of return} = \left(\begin{array}{c}\text{dividend} \\ \text{yield}\end{array}\right) \;+\; \left(\begin{array}{c}\text{growth} \\ \text{rate}\end{array}\right)$$

Study Problems

1.   The preferred stock of Craft Company pays a $3 dividend. What is the value of the stock if your required rate of return is 8%?

SOLUTION

$$\text{Value of preferred stock} = \frac{\text{dividend}}{\text{required rate of return}}$$

$$P_{ps} = \frac{\$3}{0.08} = \$37.50$$

2.   Universal Machines' common stock paid $1.50 in dividends *last year,* and dividends are expected to grow indefinitely at an annual 6% rate. What is the value of the stock if you require a 12% return?

SOLUTION

$$\text{Value } (P_{cs}) = \frac{\text{dividend in year 1}}{\text{required rate - growth rate}} = \frac{D_1}{r_{cs} - g}$$

$$\text{where } D_1 = D_0(1 + g) = \$1.50(1 + 0.06) = \$1.59$$

Then,

$$P_{cs} = \frac{\$1.59}{0.12 - 0.06} = \$26.50$$

3.   Texas Mining Company's common stock is selling for $35. The stock paid dividends of $2.50 last year and has a projected growth rate of 10%. If you buy the stock at the market price, what is the expected rate of return?

SOLUTION

Expected rate of return (k_{cs}):

$$\bar{r}_{cs} = \frac{\text{dividend in year 1}}{\text{price}} + \frac{\text{growth}}{\text{rate}} = \frac{D_1}{P_{cs}} + g$$

$$\text{where } D_1 = D_0(1 + g) = \$2.50(1 + 0.10) = \$2.75$$
$$P_0 = \$35$$
$$\bar{r}_{cs} = \frac{\$2.75}{\$35.00} + 0.10 = 0.1785$$
$$= 17.85\%$$

4.   Idalou Power Company's preferred stock is selling for $25 in the market and pays $2.50 in dividends.
   a.   What is the expected rate of return on the stock?
   b.   If your required rate of return is 12%, what is the fair value of the stock for you?
   c.   Should you acquire the stock?

SOLUTION

a. Expected rate of return $= \dfrac{\$2.50}{\$25.00} = 10\%$

b. Value of the stock to you $= \dfrac{\$2.50}{0.12} = \$20.83$

c. Since your required rate of return is higher than the expected rate of return, you should not acquire it.

5. The market price of International Electric Corporation is $40. The price at the end of one year is expected to be $45. Dividends for next year should be $2.50. What is the expected rate of return for a single holding period of one year?

SOLUTION

$$\text{current price } (P_{cs}) = \frac{\text{dividend in year 1}}{1 + \text{expected rate of return}} + \frac{\text{price in year 1}}{1 + \text{expected rate of return}}$$

$$\frac{\text{expected}}{\text{return}} = \frac{\text{dividend in year 1} + \text{price in year 1}}{\text{current price}} - 1$$

$$\frac{\text{expected}}{\text{return}} = \frac{\$2.50 + \$45.00}{\$40.00} - 1 = 18.75\%$$

Self Tests

TRUE-FALSE

_____ 1. An assumption necessary in the model for common stock valuation,

$$P_{cs} = \frac{D_1}{r_{cs} - g},$$

is that the amount of the dividend increases by a constant percent each year.

_____ 2. Protective provisions can allow preferred stockholders a voting right in the event of nonpayment of dividends.

_____ 3. If the market price of a security is larger than the value assigned to the security by an investor, then the expected rate is greater than the required rate of return.

_____ 4. The term "growth" when used in the context of a valuation model includes growth from reinvesting profits and from issuing stock.

_____ 5. The value of a preferred stock is the future value of the stock at maturity.

_____ 6. The constant growth common stock valuation model is defined as:

$$\text{common stock value} = \frac{\text{required rate of return}}{\text{dividend in year 1}},$$

assuming the dividends grow each year at a constant rate.

_____ 7. Valuation does not support the financial officer's objective of maximizing the value of the firm's common stock.

_____ 8. The option involved in convertible preferred stock belongs to the corporations issuing the shares.

_____ 9. A sinking-fund provision requires the firm to pay all unpaid preferred stock dividends before any common stock dividends are declared.

_____ 10. A cumulative feature requires the firm to set aside an amount of money for the retirement of its preferred stock.

_____ 11. The preemptive right entitles current shareholders to get the first opportunity to purchase new stock issues.

_____ 12. Preferred stockholders have a stronger voice in company operations than common stockholders do.

_____ 13. An advantage of preferred stock over common stock is that the regular interest payments must be paid before dividends can be paid to common stockholders.

_____ 14. A majority voting feature pertains to the margin by which elections must be won.

_____ 15. A proxy allows a designated party to temporarily vote for someone else.

MULTIPLE CHOICE

1.   The most recent dividend paid by Xeron on its common stock was $1.50 (annual). The required rate of return for the security is 6%. Growth is anticipated to be 4% annually. The market price of the stock should be

    a. $78.
    b. $100.
    c. $50.
    d. $150.
    e. $75.

2.   The income received by the holder of a preferred stock is similar to the income received from which other financial asset in terms of it being a constant amount each year?

    a.   common stocks
    b.   bonds
    c.   both a and b
    d.   none of the above

3. What is the expected rate of return for a stock with a current market price of $44, if the expected dividend at the conclusion of this year is $2.20, and earnings are growing at a 10% annual rate? (Assume that the dividends are anticipated to grow at the same rate.)

    a. 25%
    b. 10%
    c. 5%
    d. 15%

4. Which of the following is not a common trait of preferred stock?

    a. convertibility
    b. cumulative dividends
    c. voting rights
    d. preferred claim on assets and income over common stock

5. A _____ allows the preferred stockholder to be paid beyond the payment of the stated dividend.

    a. carry-back feature
    b. cumulative feature
    c. stock premium
    d. preemptive right

6. _____ allows the issuing corporation to retire the stock.

    a. A preemptive right
    b. Convertibility
    c. Callable preferred
    d. PIK preferred

7. Common stock involves _____ the corporation.

    a. ownership in
    b. personally managing
    c. being a creditor of
    d. the maturity of

8. _____ allow(s) a designated party the temporary power of attorney to vote for the signee at the corporation's annual meeting.

   a. Majority voting
   b. A proxy
   c. Absentee voting
   d. Protective provisions

9. _____ gives the shareholder one vote for each share of stock, and each board position is voted on separately.

   a. Cumulative voting
   b. A proxy
   c. Majority voting
   d. Preemptive right

10. Which of the following does not affect the value of a stock?

    a. expected cash inflow
    b. riskiness of the stock
    c. the investor's required rate of return
    d. the stock's par or stated value

11. Common stock dividends must be _____ before issued.

    a. approved by common stockholders
    b. registered with the SEC
    c. approved by preferred stockholders
    d. declared by the firm's board of directors

12. Common stock dividends are

    a. limited to twice the amount received by preferred stockholders.
    b. unlimited.
    c. always paid on a monthly basis.
    d. recognized before preferred stock dividends.s

CHAPTER 9

The Cost of Capital

Orientation: In Chapters 7 and 8, we considered the valuation of debt and equity securities. The concepts advanced serve as a foundation for determining the required rate of return for a firm and for specific investment projects. The objective in this chapter is to determine the required rate of return when evaluating investment projects, which is an average of the required rates of return of the creditor loaning the money to the firm and of the stockholders who own the firm.

I.   The Concept of the Cost of Capital

     A.   Defining the cost of capital:

          1.   The rate that must be earned in order to satisfy the required rate of return of the firm's investors.

          2.   The rate of return on investments at which the price of a firm's common stock will remain unchanged.

     B.   Type of investors and the cost of capital.

          1.   Each source of capital used by the firm (debt, preferred stock, and common stock) should be incorporated into the cost of capital. The relative importance of a particular source should be based on the percentage of the firm's total financing provided by that source.

          2.   Using the cost of a single source of capital as the hurdle rate for a new investment is often tempting to management where all the financing for the investment comes from that source (e.g., the retention of earnings or borrowing). This is a mistake and can lead to serious errors in the firm's investment decisions. For example, in periods when the firm is borrowing funds to finance projects the cost of debt becomes the hurdle rate whereas in periods when the firm is issuing equity they use the much higher cost of equity. Consequently, the hurdle rate varies with the source of finance the

103

firm uses and ignores the fact that the firm is actually balancing its debt and equity offerings to maintain a stable capital structure.

II. Factors Determining the Cost of Capital

A. **General economic conditions.** These include the demand for and supply of capital within the economy and the level of expected inflation. These are reflected in the riskless rate of return.

B. **Market conditions.** Not all firms can sell their debt and/or equity securities when they might want to do it. The market for equity offerings, especially for firms that have never issued equity (i.e., IPOs) is only open to new firms under very optimistic market periods. Thus, general market conditions can have an important impact on a firm's ability to raise funds at various times.

C. **A firm's operating and financing decisions.** A firm's choice of how to finance its assets and when to raise new capital is influenced by the underlying risk that investors see in the firm. In large part this risk results from the decisions made within the company and can be divided into two classes.

1. **Business risk** is the variability in returns on assets and is affected by the company's investment decisions.

2. **Financial risk** is the increased variability in firm earnings and correspondingly the returns to the common stockholders that results from the firm's use of debt and preferred stock financing as opposed to common equity.

III. Computing the weighted cost of capital. A firm's weighted cost of capital is a function of (1) the individual costs of capital and (2) the capital structure mix.

A. Determining individual costs of capital.

1. The **before-tax cost of debt** is found by solving for k_d in

$$NP_d = \sum_{t=1}^{n} \frac{\$I_t}{(1 + k_d)^t} + \frac{\$M}{(1 + k_d)^n}$$

where NP_d = the market price of the debt less flotation costs (i.e., the net proceeds from the issue)

$\$I_t$ = the annual dollar interest paid to the investor each year,

$\$M$ = the maturity value of the debt,

$$k_d \quad = \quad \text{before-tax cost of the debt (before-tax required rate of return on debt)}$$

$$n \quad = \quad \text{the number of years to maturity.}$$

The **after-tax cost of debt** equals:

$$k_d(1 - T)$$

2. Cost of preferred stock (required rate of return on preferred stock), k_{ps}, equals the dividend yield based upon the net price (market price less flotation costs) or

$$k_{ps} = \frac{\text{dividend}}{\text{net price}} = \frac{D}{NP_{ps}}$$

3. Cost of Common Stock. We use two measurement techniques to obtain estimates of the required rate of return on common stock.

   a. dividend-growth model

   b. capital asset pricing model

4. Dividend-growth model

   a. Cost of internally generated common equity, k_{cs}

   $$k_{cs} = \frac{\text{dividend in year 1}}{\text{market price}} + \left(\begin{array}{c} \text{annual growth} \\ \text{in dividends} \end{array} \right)$$

   $$k_{cs} = \frac{D_1}{P_{cs}} + g$$

   b. Cost of new common stock, k_{ncs}

   $$k_{ncs} = \frac{D_1}{P_{ncs}} + g$$

   where $NP_{cs} = $ the market price of the common stock less flotation costs incurred in issuing new shares.

5.   Capital asset pricing model

$$k_{cs} \quad = \quad k_{rf} + \beta(k_m - k_{rf})$$

where k_{cs} =   the cost of common stock

k_{rf} =   the risk-free rate

β =   beta, measure of the stock's systematic risk

k_m =   the expected rate of return on the market

6.   It is important to notice that the major difference between the equations presented here and the equations from Chapter 5 is that the **firm** incurs flotation costs when it issues any security. Thus, the cost of a particular source of capital to the firm will exceed the investor's required rate of return due to the costs of issuing the security, which are paid to investment banks and other financial intermediaries that help the firm sell its securities.

B.   **Selection of weights.** The individual costs of capital will be different for each source of capital in the firm's capital structure. To use the cost of capital in investment analyses, we must compute a weighted or overall cost of capital.

1.   We have assumed that the company's current financial mix resulting from the financing of previous investments is relatively stable and that these weights will closely approximate future financing patterns.

2.   In computing weights, a question arises as to whether we should use current market values of the firm's securities or the book values as shown in the balance sheet. Since we will be issuing new securities at their **current** market value, and not at book (historical) values, we should use the market value of the securities in calculating our weights.

IV.   PepsiCo Approach to Weighted Average Cost of Capital

A.   PepsiCo calculates the divisional cost of capital for its snack, beverage, and restaurant organizations by first finding peer-group firms for each division and using their average betas, after adjusting for differences in financial leverage, to compute the division's cost of equity. They also use accounting betas in estimating the cost of equity. They then compute the cost of debt for each division. Finally, they calculate a weighted cost of capital for each division.

B.   PepsiCo's WACC basic computation

$$k_{wacc} = k_{cs}\left(\frac{E}{D+E}\right) + k_d[1\text{-}T]\left(\frac{D}{D+E}\right)$$

where:

k_{wacc}	=	the weighted average cost of capital
k_{cs}	=	the cost of equity capital
k_d	=	the before-tax cost of debt capital
T_c	=	the firm's tax rate
E/(D+E)	=	percentage of financing from equity
D/(D+E)	=	percentage of financing from debt

C.   Calculating the Cost of Equity

Based on capital assets pricing model:

$$k_{cs} = k_{rf} + \beta (k_m - k_{rf})$$

where:

k_{cs}	=	the cost of common stock
k_{rf}	=	the risk-free rate
β	=	beta, measure of the stock's systematic risk
k_m	=	the expected rate of return on the market

Betas for each division are estimated by calculating an average unlevered beta from a group of divisional peers.

The average beta for each division's peer group is adjusted so that it reflects the division's target debt-to-equity ratio.

D.   Calculating the Cost of Debt

The after-tax cost of debt is equal to:

$k_d (1 - T_c)$

where:

k_d	=	before-tax cost of debt
T_c	=	marginal tax rate

Study Problems

1. A $1,000 par-value bond will sell in the market for $1,072 and carries a coupon interest rate of 9%. Issuance costs will be 7.5%. The number of years to maturity is .15, and the firm's tax rate is 46%. What is the after-tax cost for this security (K_d)?

SOLUTION

Use your financial calculator following the procedure on page 366 to calculate $K_d = 9.11\%$.

2. The current market price of ABC Company's common stock is $32.50. The firm expects to pay a dividend of $1.90, and the growth rate is projected to be 7% annually. The company is in a 40% tax bracket. Flotation costs would be 6% if new stock were issued. What is the cost of (a) internal and (b) external common equity?

SOLUTION

Let k_{cs}	=	cost of internal common
k_{ncs}	=	cost of external (new) common
D_1	=	next dividend to be paid
P_{cs}	=	market price
g	=	growth rate
NP_o	=	market price less flotation costs

(a) $k_{cs} = \dfrac{D_1}{P_o} + g$

$$k_{cs} = \frac{\$1.90}{\$32.50} + 0.07 = 12.85\%$$

(b) $k_{ns} = \dfrac{D_1}{NP_o} + g$

$$k_{ncs} = \frac{\$1.90}{\$32.50(1-0.06)} + 0.07 = 13.22\%$$

3.	Pharr, Inc.'s preferred stock pays a 16% dividend. The stock is selling for $62.75, and its par value is $40. Issuance costs are 5% and the firm's tax rate is 46%. What is the cost of this source of financing?

SOLUTION

$$k_{ps} = \frac{D}{NP_o}$$

$$k_{ps} = \frac{\$40(0.16)}{\$62.75(1-0.05)} = \frac{\$6.40}{\$59.61} = 10.74\%$$

4.	The current capital structure of Smithhart, Inc. is as follows:

Bonds (7%, $1,000 par, 15 years)	$ 750,000	
Preferred stock ($100 par, 7.25% dividend)	1,000,000	
Common stock:		
Par value ($2.50 par)	$500,000	
Retained earnings	350,000	850,000
Total		$2,600,000

The market price is $975 for the bonds, $60 for the preferred stock, and $21 for common stocks. Flotation costs are 9% for bonds and 5 percent for preferred stock. The firm's tax rate is 46%. Common stock will pay a $2.80 dividend, which is not expected to grow. What is the weighted cost of capital using only internal common equity?

SOLUTION

Source of Financing	Market Value	Weight
Bonds	$731,250[1]	13.22%
Preferred stock	600,000[2]	10.85%
Common stock	4,200,000[3]	75.93%
	$5,531,250	100.00%

[1] 750 bonds at $975 value each

[2] 10, 000 shares at $60 value each

[3] 200, 000 shares at $21 value each

Cost of debt

$$\$975(1-0.09) \text{ or } \$887.25 = \sum_{t=1}^{15}\frac{\$70}{(1+k_d)}t + \frac{\$1,000}{(1+k_d)}15$$

Using a financial calculator, k_d equals 8.35%.

$$k_d = 8.35\% \ (1-0.46)$$

$$k_d = 4.51\%$$

Cost of preferred stock

$$k_{ps} = \frac{\$7.25}{\$60(1-0.05)} = 12.72\%$$

Cost of internal common equity

$$k_{cs} = \frac{\$2.80}{\$21} + 0 = 13.33\%$$

Weighted Cost of Capital

Source of Financing	Cost	Weight	Weighted Costs
Bonds	4.51%	.1322	0.596%
Preferred stock	12.72	.1085	1.381
Common stock	13.33	.7593	10.124
			12.101%

Self Tests

TRUE-FALSE

_____ 1. The cost of capital is defined as the rate of return that the firm must earn on its investments if the investments are to leave the price of the firm's common stock unchanged.

_____ 2. Book values from the firm's balance sheet should be used when calculating a firm's weighted average cost of capital.

_____ 3. The firm's cost of capital is an appropriate investment hurdle only for investments whose risk is similar risk to that of existing assets.

_____ 4. Financial risk is the risk that the price of a bond or stock may vary over time.

_____ 5. Only those projects with an expected return equal to or exceeding the cost of capital should be accepted.

_____ 6. The cost of preferred stock, like the cost of debt, must be adjusted for taxes.

_____ 7. In using a firm's weighted average cost of capital to evaluate new investments, we are assuming that the company's current capital structure will not change over the life of the investment.

_____ 8. As a general rule, new common stock is issued only if internal common equity (retained earnings) does not provide sufficient equity capital.

_____ 9. The capital asset pricing model (CAPM) is based on three variables: the risk-free rate, the firm's beta coefficient, and the market risk premium.

_____ 10. The beta for a firm's common stock measures the volatility of the project returns relative to that of a widely diversified portfolio of all other risky assets.

MULTIPLE CHOICE

1. What is/are the reason(s) for computing a firm's cost of capital?

    a. to determine the firm's future financing needs
    b. to assure the investors that their required rate of return is being met
    c. to use the cost of capital as an investment criterion
    d. b and c
    e. a and c
    f. a, b, and c

2. The cost of capital can be defined as

    a. the rate that must be earned in order to satisfy the required rate of return of the firm's investors.
    b. the rate of return on investments at which the price of the firm's common stock remains unchanged.
    c. the rate of return on investments that will increase the price of the firm's common stock.
    d. a and b.
    e. a and c.

3. All *except* which of the following variables are required to compute the cost of debt?

    a. the market price of debt
    b. issuance or flotation costs
    c. the tax rate for the firm
    d. the growth rate in future dividends
    e. the principal amount of the debt issue

4. Adjustment for taxes is required for estimating which of the following?

    a. cost of preferred stock
    b. cost of debt
    c. cost of common equity
    d. cost of retained earnings
    e. all of the above

5.   An investment with a beta of 0.80 means that the returns of the investment

     a.   are more volatile than market returns.
     b.   are less volatile than market returns.
     c.   have no correlation with the market returns.
     d.   are perfectly correlated with the market returns.
     e.   None of the above are true.

6.   Firms that operate in two or more businesses that differ in their business risk
     (e.g., an oil and gas exploration unit and a petroleum refining unit) should

     a.   use a single company-wide cost of capital to evaluate new investment
          opportunities in either of its business units.
     b.   evaluate the individual costs of capital for each business unit and use the
          different costs to evaluate each unit.
     c.   ignore the different business units as investors can only purchase stock in
          the company as a whole.
     d.   Both a and c are correct.
     e.   None of the above are correct.

7.   The appropriate set of weights used in calculating a firm's weighted average
     cost of capital should reflect

     a.   the sources of financing the firm has used in its capital structure.
     b.   the mix of financing sources used to fund the particular set of projects
          being analyzed.
     c.   the average mix of financing sources reflected in the firm's current
          balance sheet.
     d.   all of the above.
     e.   none of the above.

8.   When firms operate in multiple industries for which the risk characteristics and
     financial structures vary significantly, they should

     a.   use a company-wide weighted average cost of capital to evaluate all new
          investments so as to hold each operating division to the same standard.
     b.   calculate divisional costs of capital for use in evaluating each division's
          investment opportunities.
     c.   try to adjust the capital structures used in each of the divisions such that
          the weighted average cost of capital in each is the same.
     d.   All of the above are true.
     e.   None of the above are true.

9. The cost of common equity is more difficult to estimate than the cost of bonds or preferred stock because

    a. common dividends are not contractually specified and must be estimated.
    b. common equity does not have a finite maturity like debt.
    c. common equity can be raised from two sources: the retention of earnings and the issuance of new common shares.
    d. All of the above are true.
    e. None of the above are true.

10. The dividend growth model estimates the cost of common equity as

    a. the sum of the current dividend yield and the anticipated rate of growth in future dividends.
    b. the sum of the risk-free rate of interest and a market risk premium.
    c. the reciprocal of the firm's price to earnings ratio.
    d. all of the above.
    e. none of the above.

CHAPTER 10

Capital-Budgeting Techniques and Practice

<u>Orientation</u>: Capital budgeting involves the decision-making process with respect to investment in fixed assets; specifically, it involves measuring the incremental cash flows associated with investment proposals, then evaluating the attractiveness of these cash flows relative to the project's costs. This chapter focuses on the various decision criteria. It also examines how to deal with complications in the capital-budgeting process including mutually exclusive projects and capital rationing.

I. Methods for Evaluating Projects

    A. The payback period method

        1. The payback period of an investment tells the number of years required to recover the initial investment. The payback period is calculated by adding the cash flows up until they are equal to the initial fixed investment.

        2. Although this measure does, in fact, deal with cash flows and is easy to calculate and understand, it ignores any cash flows that occur after the payback period and does not consider the time value of money within the payback period.

        3. To deal with the criticism that the payback period ignores the time value of money some firms use the discounted payback period. The discounted payback period method is similar to the traditional payback period except that it uses discounted net cash flows rather than actual undiscounted net cash flows in calculating the payback period.

        4. The discounted payback period is defined as the number of years needed to recover the initial cash outlay from the discounted net cash flows.

B.　　Present-value methods

    1.　　The net present value of an investment project is the present value of the cash inflows less the present value of the cash outflows. By assigning negative values to cash outflows, it becomes

$$NPV = \sum_{t=1}^{n} \frac{FCF_t}{(1+k)^t} - IO$$

    where FCFt　=　the annual free cash flow in time period t (this can take on either positive or negative values)

        k　=　the required rate of return or appropriate discount rate or cost of capital

        IO　=　the initial cash outlay

        n　=　the project's expected life

    a.　　The acceptance criteria are

        accept if NPV $\geq$ 0

        reject if NPV $<$ 0

    b.　　The advantage of this approach is that it takes the time value of money into consideration in addition to dealing with cash flows.

    2.　　The profitability index is the ratio of the present value of the expected future net cash flows to the initial cash outlay, or

$$\text{profitability index} = \frac{\sum_{t=1}^{n} \frac{FCF_t}{(1+k)^t}}{IO}$$

    a.　　The acceptance criteria are

        accept if PI $\geq$ 1.0

        reject if PI $<$ 1.0

    b.　　The advantages of this method are the same as those for the net present value.

    c.　　Either of these present-value methods will give the same accept/reject decisions to a project.

C.　　The internal rate of return is the discount rate that equates the present value of the project's future net cash flows with the project's initial outlay. Thus the internal rate of return is represented by IRR in the equation below:

$$IO = \sum_{t=1}^{n} \frac{FCF_t}{(1 + IRR)^t}$$

1.   The acceptance-rejection criteria are:

   accept if IRR ≥ required rate of return

   reject if IRR < required rate of return

   The required rate of return is often taken to be the firm's cost of capital.

2.   The advantages of this method are that it deals with cash flows and recognizes the time value of money; however, the procedure is rather complicated and time consuming.

D.   The MIRR is similar to the IRR except it relies on the assumption that all free cash flows over the life of the project are reinvested at the required rate of return until the termination of the project. Thus, to calculate the *MIRR*, we:

Step 1: Determine the present value of the project's free cash *out*flows. We do this by discounting all the free cash *out*flows, back to the present at the required rate of return. If the initial outlay is the only free cash *out*flow, then the initial outlay is the present value of the free cash *out*flows.

Step 2: Determine the present value of the project's free cash inflows. Take all the annual free cash *in*flows and find their future value at the end of the project's life, compounded forward at the required rate of return. We will call this the project's *terminal value*, or *TV*.

Step 3: Calculate the MIRR. The MIRR is the discount rate that equates the present value of the free cash outflows with the present value of the project's terminal value.

1.   The modified internal rate of return is defined as the value of MIRR in the following equation:

$$PV_{outflows} = \frac{TV_{inflows}}{(1 + MIRR)^n} \qquad (10\text{-}4)$$

Where $PV_{outflows}$ = the present value of the project's free cash outflows

$TV_{inflows}$ = the project's terminal value, calculated by taking all the annual free cash *in*flows and find their future value at the end of the project's life, compounded forward at the required rate of return

n = the project's expected life

MIRR = the project's modified internal rate of return

E. The easiest way to understand the relationship between the IRR and the NPV is to view it graphically through the use of a net present value profile. A net present value profile is simply a graph showing how a project's NPV changes as the discount rate changes. From the net present value profile you can easily see how a project's NPV varies inversely with the discount rate, and you can also see how sensitive the project is to your selection of the discount rate.

II. Mutually exclusive projects: Although the IRR and the present-value methods will, in general, give consistent accept-reject decisions, they may not rank projects identically. This becomes important in the case of mutually exclusive projects.

A. A project is mutually exclusive if acceptance of it precludes the acceptance of one or more possible projects. Then, in this case, the project's relative ranking becomes important.

B. Ranking conflicts come as a result of the different assumptions on the reinvestment rate on funds released from the proposals. The MIRR method can take care of this problem.

C. Thus, when conflicting ranking of mutually exclusive projects results from the different reinvestment assumptions, the decision boils down to which assumption is best.

D. In general, the net present value method is considered to be theoretically superior.

III. Capital rationing is the situation in which a budget ceiling or constraint is placed upon the amount of funds that can be invested during a time period.

    A. Theoretically, a firm should never reject a project that yields more than the required rate of return. Although there are circumstances that may create complicated situations, in general, an investment policy limited by capital rationing is less than optimal.

IV. Without question, the key to success in capital budgeting is identifying good projects, and for many companies these good projects are overseas. In fact, Coca-Cola, Xerox, Hewlett-Packard, and IBM all earn more than 50% of their profits from abroad.

Study Problems

1. The cost of new machinery for a given investment project will be $100,000. Incremental cash flows after taxes will be $40,000 in years 1 and 2 and will be $60,000 in year 3. What is the payback period for this project, and if acceptable projects must recover the initial investment in 2.5 years, should this project be accepted or rejected?

SOLUTION

After two years they will have recovered $80,000 of the $100,000 outlay and they expect to recover an additional $60,000 in the third year. Thus, the payback period becomes

$$2 \text{ years} + \frac{\$20,000}{\$60,000} = 2.33 \text{ years}$$

2.33 years < 2.5 years. Therefore, accept the project.

2. A given investment project will cost $50,000. Incremental annual cash flows after taxes are expected to be $10,000 per year for the life of the investment, which is five years. There will be no salvage value at the end of the five years. The required rate of return is 14%. On the basis of the profitability index method, should the investment be accepted?

SOLUTION

PV of cash flow = $10,000(3.433) = $34,330

PV of cash outlay = $50,000

$$PI = \frac{\$34,330}{\$50,000} = 0.6866 < 1$$

Therefore, the project should be rejected.

3. Determine the internal rate of return on the following projects:

(a) An initial outlay of $10,000 resulting in a cash flow of $2,146 at the end of each year for the next 10 years

(b) An initial outlay of $10,000 resulting in a cash flow of $1,960 at the end of each year for the next 20 years

(c) An initial outlay of $10,000 resulting in a cash flow of $1,396 at the end of each year for the next 12 years

(d) An initial outlay of $10,000 resulting in a cash flow of $3,197 at the end of each year for the next five years

SOLUTION

(a) N   =   10
     CPT I/Y =   17
     PV   =   -10,000
     PMT   =   2,146
     FV   =   0

(b)

N	=	20
CPT I/Y =		**19**
PV	=	-10,000
PMT	=	1,960
FV	=	0

(c)

N	=	12
CPT I/Y =		**9**
PV	=	-10,000
PMT	=	1,396
FV	=	0

(d)

N	=	5
CPT I/Y =		**18**
PV	=	-10,000
PMT	=	3,197
FV	=	0

4. The Battling Bishops Corporation is considering two mutually exclusive pieces of machinery that perform the same task. The two available alternatives provide the following set of after-tax net cash flows:

Year	Equipment A	Equipment B
0	–$20,000	–$20,000
1	13,000	6,500
2	13,000	6,500
3	13,000	6,500
4		6,500
5		6,500
6		6,500
7		6,500
8		6,500
9		6,500

Equipment A has an expected life of three years, whereas equipment B has an expected life of nine years. Assume a required rate of return of 14%.

(a) Calculate each project's payback period.

(b) Calculate each project's net present value.

(c) Calculate each project's internal rate of return.

(d) Are these projects comparable?

(e) Compare these projects using replacement chains and EAAs. Which project should be selected? Support your recommendation.

SOLUTION

(a) Payback A = 1.5385 years

Payback B = 3.0769 years

(b) NPV_A = $\displaystyle\sum_{t=1}^{3} \frac{\$13,000}{(1 + 0.14)^t} - \$20,000$

= $\$13,000\ (2.322) - \$20,000$

= $\$30,186 - \$20,000$

= $\$10,186$

NPV_B = $\displaystyle\sum_{t=1}^{9} \frac{\$6,500}{(1 + 0.14)^t} - \$20,000$

= $\$6,500\ (4.946) - \$20,000$

= $\$32,149 - \$20,000$

= $\$12,149$

(c) Project A:

N = 3

CPT I/Y = **42.57**

PV = -20,000

PMT = 13,000

FV = 0

Project B:

N = 9

CPT I/Y = **29.28**

PV = -20,000

PMT = 6,500

FV = 0

(d)   These projects are not comparable because future profitable investment proposals are affected by the decision currently being made. If project A is taken, at its termination the firm could replace the machine and receive additional benefits, while acceptance of project B would exclude this possibility.

(e)   Using three replacement chains, project A's cash flows would become:

Year	Cash flow
0	-$20,000
1	13,000
2	13,000
3	– 7,000
4	13,000
5	13,000
6	– 7,000
7	13,000
8	13,000
9	13,000

$$NPV_A = \sum_{t=1}^{9} \frac{\$13,000}{(1 + 0.14)^t} - \$20,000 - \frac{\$20,000}{(1+0.14)^3} - \frac{\$20,000}{(1+0.14)^6}$$

$$= \quad \$13,000(4.946) - \$20,000 - \$20,000\,(0.675)$$

$$- \$20,000\,(0.456)$$

$$= \quad \$64,298 - \$20,000 - \$13,500 - \$9,120$$

$$= \quad \$21,678$$

The replacement chain analysis indicated that project A should be selected, as the replacement chain associated with it has a larger NPV than project B.

Project A's EAA:

Step 1: Calculate the project's NPV (from part b):

$NPV_A = \$10,186$

Step 2: Calculate the EAA:

$$EAA_A = NPV / PVIFA_{14\%, \text{ 3 yr.}}$$

$$= \$10,186 / 2.322$$

$$= \$4,387$$

Project B's EAA:

Step 1: Calculate the project's NPV (from part b):

$$NPV_B = \$12,149$$

Step 2: Calculate the EAA:

$$EAA_B = NPV / PVIFA_{14\%, \text{ 9 yr.}}$$

$$= \$12,149 / 4.946$$

$$= \$2,256$$

Project B should be selected because it has a higher EAA.

Self Tests

TRUE-FALSE

_____ 1.   Capital rationing occurs because profitable projects must be rejected based on a lack of capital.

_____ 2.   The net present value of a project decreases as the required rate of return increases.

_____ 3.   The higher the discount rate, the more valued is the proposal with the early cash flows, all else being equal.

_____ 4.   The net present value of a project will equal zero whenever the profitability index equals 1.0.

_____ 5.   The net present value of a project will equal zero whenever the payback period of a project equals the firm's required payback period.

_____ 6.   Capital rationing is not an optimal capital-budgeting strategy.

_____ 7. The profitability index provides the same accept/reject decision result as the net present value method.

_____ 8. If two projects are mutually exclusive, the one with the highest expected value should always be chosen, even if it is riskier.

_____ 9. One difference between the NPV and IRR approaches is the reinvestment rate assumption.

_____ 10. For mutually exclusive projects, the NPV approach is preferred over the profitability index because the NPV measures worth in absolute terms while the PI measures worth in relative terms.

MULTIPLE CHOICE

1. Which of the following considers the time value of money?

    a. payback method
    b. return on investment
    c. profitability index
    d. none of the above

2. Which of the following is a non-discounted cash flow approach?

    a. payback period
    b. profitability index
    c. internal rate of return
    d. net present value

3. If the internal rate of return is greater than the required rate of return,

    a. the present value of all the cash flows will be less than the initial outlay.
    b. the payback will be less than the life of the investment.
    c. the project should be accepted.
    d. a and c.

4. If the cash flow pattern for a project has two sign reversals, then there can be as many as _____ positive IRRs.

    a.   1
    b.   2
    c.   3
    d.   4

CHAPTER 11

Cash Flows and Other Topics in Capital Budgeting

<u>Orientation</u>: Capital budgeting involves the decision-making process with respect to investment in fixed assets; specifically, it involves measuring the incremental cash flows associated with investment proposals and evaluating the attractiveness of these cash flows relative to the project's costs. This chapter focuses on the estimation of those cash flows based on various decision criteria and how to adjust for the riskiness of a given project or combination of projects.

I.   What criteria should we use in the evaluation of alternative investment proposals?

   A.   Use cash flows rather than accounting profits, because cash flows allow us to analyze the time element of the flows correctly.

   B.   Examine cash flows on an after-tax basis because they are the flows available to shareholders.

   C.   Include only the incremental cash flows resulting from the investment decision. Ignore all other flows.

II.   Measuring free cash flows. We are interested in measuring the incremental after-tax cash flows, or free cash flows, resulting from the investment proposal. In general, there will be three major sources of cash flows: initial outlays, differential cash flows over the project's life, and terminal cash flows.

   A.   Initial outlays include whatever cash flows are necessary to get the project in running order, for example:

      1.   The installed cost of the asset.

2. In the case of a replacement proposal, the selling price of the old machine plus (or minus) any tax gain (or loss) offsetting the initial outlay.

3. Any expense items (for example, training) necessary for the operation of the proposal.

4. Any other non-expense cash outlays required, such as increased working-capital needs.

B. Differential cash flows over the project's life include the incremental after-tax flows over the life of the project, for example:

1. Added revenue (less added selling expenses) for the proposal.

2. Any labor and/or material savings incurred.

3. Increases in overhead incurred.

4. Changes in taxes.

5. Change in net working capital.

6. Change in capital spending.

7. Make sure calculations reflect the fact that while depreciation is an expense, it does not involve any cash flows.

8. A word of warning not to include financing charges (such as interest or preferred stock dividends), for they are implicitly taken care of in the discounting process.

C. Terminal cash flows include any incremental cash flows that result at the termination of the project; for example:

1. The project's salvage value plus (or minus) any taxable gains or losses associated with the project.

2. Any terminal cash flow needed, and perhaps disposal of obsolete equipment.

3. Recovery of any non-expense cash outlays associated with the project, such as recovery of increased working-capital needs associated with the proposal.

III. Measuring the cash flows.

    A. A project's free cash flows =

        project's change in operating cash flows

        - change in net working capital

        - change in capital spending

    B If we rewrite this, inserting the calculations for the project's change in operating cash flows, we get:

        A project's free cash flows =

        Change in earnings before interest and taxes

        - change in taxes

        + change in depreciation

        - change in net working capital

        - change in capital spending

IV. Options in Capital Budgeting. Options in capital budgeting are ways to deal with the opportunity to modify a project. Three of the most common types of options that can add value to a capital budgeting project are: (1) the option to delay a project until the future cash flows are more favorable—this option is common when the firm has exclusive rights, perhaps a patent, to a product or technology; (2) the option to expand a project, perhaps in size or even to new products that would not have otherwise been feasible; and (3) the option to abandon a project if the future cash flows fall short of expectations.

V. Risk and the Investment Decision

    A. Up to this point, we have treated the expected cash flows resulting from an investment proposal as being known with perfect certainty. We will now introduce risk.

    B. The riskiness of an investment project is defined as the variability of its cash flows from the expected cash flow.

VI. Incorporating Risk into Capital Budgeting

A. The use of the risk-adjusted discount rate is based on the concept that investors demand higher returns for more risky projects.

1. If the risk associated with the investment is greater than the risk involved in a typical endeavor, then the discount rate is adjusted upward to compensate for this risk.

2. The expected cash flows are then discounted back to the present at the risk-adjusted discount rate. Then the normal capital-budgeting criteria are applied, except in the case of the internal rate of return, in which case the hurdle rate to which the project's internal rate of return is compared now becomes the risk-adjusted discount rate.

3. Expressed mathematically, the net present value using the risk-adjusted discount rate becomes

$$NPV = \sum_{t=1}^{n} \frac{FCF_t}{(1 + k^*)^t} - IO$$

where FCF_t = the annual free

k^* = the risk-adjusted discount rate

n = the project's expected life

VII. Methods for Measuring a Project's Systematic Risk

A. Theoretically, we know that systematic risk is the "priced" risk, the risk that affects the stock's market price, and the appropriate risk with which to be concerned. However, if there are bankruptcy costs (which are assumed away by the CAPM), if there are undiversified shareholders who are concerned with more than just systematic risk, if there are factors that affect a security's price beyond what the CAPM suggests, or if we are unable to measure the project's systematic risk confidently, then the project's individual risk carries relevance. In general, a project's individual risk is highly correlated with the project's systematic risk making it a reasonable proxy to use.

B. In spite of problems in confidently measuring an individual firm's level of systematic risk, if the project appears to be typical for the firm, then using the CAPM to determine the appropriate risk-return trade-offs and judging the project against them may be a warranted approach.

C.   If the project is not a typical project, we are without historical data and must either estimate the beta using accounting data or use the pure-play method for estimating beta.

   1.   Using historical accounting data to substitute for historical price data in estimating systematic risk: To estimate a project's beta using accounting data we need only run a time series regression of the division's return on assets on the market index. The regression coefficient from this equation would be the project's accounting beta and serves as an approximation for the project's true beta.

   2.   The pure-play method for estimating a project's beta: The pure-play method attempts to find a publicly traded firm in the same industry as the capital-budgeting project. Once the proxy or pure-play firm is identified, its systematic risk is determined and then used as a proxy for the project's systematic risk.

VIII.   Examining a Project's Risk Through Simulation

A.   A simulation imitates the performance of the project being evaluated by randomly selecting observations from each of the distributions that affect the outcome of the project, combining those observations to determine the final output of the final project, and continuing with this process until a representative record of the project's probable outcome is assembled.

   1.   The firm's management then examines the resultant probability distribution, and if management believes enough of the distribution lies above the normal cutoff criterion, it will accept the project.

   2.   The use of a simulation approach to analyze investment proposals offers two major advantages:

      a.   The financial managers are able to examine and base their decisions on the whole range of possible outcomes rather than just point estimates.

      b.   They can undertake subsequent sensitivity analysis of the project.

IX.   The multinational dimension of business not only makes the calculation of cash flows more difficult, but it also increases the risk that a firm faces.

Study Problems

1. The R. T. Kleinman Corporation is considering selling one of its old assembly machines. The machine, purchased for $40,000 five years ago, had an expected life of 10 years and an expected salvage value of 0. Assume Kleinman uses simplified, straight-line depreciation, creating depreciation of $4,000 per year, and could sell this old machine for $45,000. Also assume a 34% marginal tax rate.

    (a) What would be the taxes associated with this sale?

    (b) If the old machine were sold for $40,000, what would be the taxes associated with this sale?

    (c) If the old machine were sold for $20,000, what would be the taxes associated with this sale?

    (d) If the old machine were sold for $17,000, what would be the taxes associated with this sale?

SOLUTION

    (a) Tax payments associated with the sale for $45,000:

    Recapture of depreciation

$$= (\$45,000 - \$20,000)\,(0.34) = \$8,500$$

    (b) Tax payments associated with sale for $40,000:

    Recapture of depreciation

$$= (\$40,000 - \$20,000)\,(0.34) = \$6,800$$

    (c) No taxes, because the machine would have been sold for its book value.

    (d) Tax savings from sale below book value:

    Tax savings $= (\$20,000 - \$17,000)\,(0.34) = \$1,020$

2.   The G. Wolfe Corporation is introducing a new product and which is expected to result in change in EBIT of $900,000. The firm has a 34 percent marginal tax rate. This product will also produce $200,000 of depreciation per year. In addition, this product will cause the following changes:

	Without the product	With the product
Accounts receivable	$60,000	$70,000
Inventory	55,000	65,000
Accounts payable	45,000	50,000

What is the product's free cash flow?

SOLUTION

Initial Outlay

Change in net working capital equals the increase in accounts receivable and inventory less the increase in accounts receivable = $10,000 + $10,000 − $5,000 = $15,000.

The change in taxes will be EBIT X marginal tax rate = $900,000 x .34 = $306,000.

A project's free cash flows =

Change in earnings before interest and taxes

−   change in taxes

+   change in depreciation

−   change in net working capital

−   change in capital spending

= $900,000
− $306,000
+ $200,000
− $15,000
−− $0
= $779,000

3. A firm is considering introducing a new product that has an expected life of five years. Since this product is much riskier than a typical project for this firm, the management feels that the normal required rate of return of 12% is not sufficient; instead, the minimally acceptable rate of return on this project should be 20%. The initial outlay would be $100,000, and the expected cash flows from this project are as given below.

Year	Expected Cash Flow
1	$40,000
2	40,000
3	40,000
4	40,000
5	40,000

Should this project be accepted?

SOLUTION

Discounting this annuity back to present at 20% yields a present value of the future cash flows of $119,640. Since the initial outlay on this project is $100,000, the net present value becomes $19,640. The project should be accepted.

Self Tests

TRUE-FALSE

_____ 1. Cash flow, not income, is what is important in capital budgeting.

_____ 2. One way of evaluating risky projects is by discounting the expected cash flows at a risk-adjusted discount rate.

_____ 3. The interest payments should be subtracted from the cash flows in evaluating projects financed with debt.

_____ 4. While depreciation is not a cash flow item, it affects taxes, which are a cash flow item.

_____ 5. Any changes in inventory or working capital need not be considered in capital budgeting because these cash flows never leave the firm.

_____ 6.   Other things held constant, the use of accelerated depreciation causes profits to be less in the earlier years; therefore in the earlier years, taxes are lower, and cash flows are higher.

_____ 7.   The use of risk-adjusted discount rates is based on the concept that investors require a higher rate of return for more risky projects.

_____ 8.   As the salvage value of the equipment being replaced increases, all else held constant, the net present value of the project will increase.

MULTIPLE CHOICE

1.   Which of the following is not a method for adjusting for or measuring risk in capital budgeting?

    a.   simulation
    b.   risk-adjusted discount rate
    c.   inverse profitability index

2.   An investment project will be more desirable

    a.   the smaller the standard deviation.
    b.   the less positive its correlations with existing average cash flows.
    c.   the larger the coefficient of variation of its cash flow.
    d.   a and b are both true.

3.   Which of the following is important to capital budgeting decisions?

    a.   depreciation method
    b.   salvage value
    c.   timing of cash flows
    d.   taxes
    e.   all of the above.

4.   If the federal income tax rate were increased, the result would be to

    a.   decrease the net present value.
    b.   increase the net present value.
    c.   increase the payback period.
    d.   cause both a and c.

CHAPTER 12

Determining the Financing Mix

Orientation: This chapter focuses on useful aids to the financial manager in his or her determination of the firm's proper financial structure. It includes the definitions of the different kinds of risk, a review of break-even analysis, the concepts of operating leverage, financial leverage, the combination of both leverages, and their effect on EPS (earnings per share). Then the chapter concentrates on the way the firm arranges its sources of funds. The cost of capital-capital structure argument is highlighted in a straightforward manner without dwelling excessively on pure theory. A moderate view of the effect of financial leverage on the firm's overall cost of capital is highlighted and explained. Later, techniques useful to the financial officer faced with the determination of an appropriate financing mix are described. Agency theory and the concept of free cash flow as both relate to capital structure determination are also discussed. An overview of actual practice is also included.

I.   Business Risk and Financial Risk

    A.   Risk has been defined as the likely variability associated with expected revenue streams.

        1.   Focusing on the financial decision, the variations in the income stream can be attributed to:

            a.   The firm's exposure to business risk.

            b.   The firm's decision to incur financial risk.

    B.   Business risk can be defined as the variability of the firm's expected earnings before interest and taxes (EBIT).

        1.   Business risk is measured by the firm's corresponding expected coefficient of variation (i.e., the larger the ratio, the more risk a firm is exposed to).

2.   Dispersion in operating income does not cause business risk. It is the result of several influences, for example, the company's cost structure, product demand characteristics, and intra-industry competition. These influences are a direct result of the firm's investment decision.

C.   Financial risk is a direct result of the firm's financing decision. When the firm is selecting different financial alternatives, financial risk refers to the additional variability in earnings available to the firm's common shareholders and the additional chance of insolvency caused by the use of financial leverage and borne by the common shareholders.

    1.   Financial leverage is the financing of a portion of the firm's assets with securities bearing a fixed (limited) rate of return in hopes of increasing the ultimate return to the common share-holders.

    2.   Financial risk, is to a large extent, passed on to the common shareholders who must bear almost all of the potential inconsistencies of returns to the firm after the deduction of fixed payments.

II.   Break-even Analysis

A.   The objective of break-even analysis is to determine the break-even quantity of output by studying the relationships among the firm's cost structure, volume of output, and operating profit.

    1.   The break-even quantity of output is the quantity of output (in units) that results in an EBIT level equal to zero.

B.   Use of the model enables the financial officer to:

    1.   Determine the quantity of output that must be sold to cover all operating costs.

    2.   Calculate the EBIT that will be achieved at various output levels.

C.   Some actual and potential applications of break-even analysis include:

    1.   Capital expenditure analysis as a complementary technique to discounted cash flow evaluation models.

    2.   Pricing policy.

    3.   Labor contract negotiations.

    4.   Evaluation of cost structure.

    5.   The making of financial decisions.

D. Essential elements of the break-even model are:

1. Fixed costs are costs that do not vary in total amount as the sales volume or the quantity of output changes over some relevant range of output. For example, administrative salaries are considered fixed because these salaries are generally the same month after month. Other examples are:

   a. Depreciation.

   b. Insurance premiums.

   c. Property taxes.

   d. Rent.

   The total fixed cost is unchanged regardless of the quantity of product output or sales, although, over some relevant range, these costs may be higher or lower (i.e., in the long run).

2. Variable costs are costs that tend to vary in total as output changes. Variable costs are fixed per unit of output. For example, direct materials are considered a variable cost because they vary with the amount of products produced. Other variable costs are:

   a. Direct labor.

   b. Energy cost associated with the production area.

   c. Packaging.

   d. Freight-out.

   e. Sales commissions.

3. To implement the behavior of the break-even model, it is necessary for the financial manager to:

   a. Identify the most relevant output range for his or her planning purposes.

   b. Approximate all costs in the semifixed–semivariable range and allocate them to the fixed and variable cost categories.

4. Total revenue and volume of output

   a. Total revenue from sales is equal to the price per unit multiplied by the quantity sold.

   b. The volume of output is the firm's level from operations and is expressed as sales dollars or a unit quantity.

E.   Finding the break-even point

    1.   The break-even model is just a simple adaptation of the firm's income statement expressed in the following format:

        sales – (total variable costs + total fixed costs) = profit

        a.   Trial and error

            (1)   Select an arbitrary output level.

            (2)   Calculate the corresponding EBIT amount.

            (3)   When EBIT equals zero, the break-even point has been found.

        b.   Contribution margin analysis

            (1)   The difference between the unit selling price and the unit variable cost equals the contribution margin.

            (2)   Then, the fixed cost divided by the contribution margin equals the break-even quantity in units.

        c.   Algebraic analysis

            (1) Q_B = the break-even level of units sold,

                P = the unit sales price,

                F = the total fixed cost for the period,

                V = unit variable cost.

            (2)   Then,

$$Q_B = \frac{F}{P - V}$$

F.   The break-even point in sales dollars:

    1.   Computing a break-even point in terms of sales dollars rather than units of output is convenient, especially if the firm deals with more than one product. Also, if the analyst cannot get unit cost data, he or she can compute a general break-even point in sales dollars by using the firm's annual report.

    2.   Since variable cost per unit and the selling price per unit are assumed constant, the ratio of total sales to total variable costs

(VC/S) is a constant for any level of sales. So, if the break-even level of sales is denoted S*, the corresponding equation is:

$$S^* = \frac{F}{1 - \dfrac{VC}{S}}$$

G. Limitations of break-even analysis:

1. The cost-volume-profit relationship is assumed to be linear.

2. The total revenue curve is presumed to increase linearly with the volume of output.

3. A constant production and sales mix is assumed.

4. The break-even computation is a static form of analysis.

III. Operating Leverage

A. Operating leverage is the responsiveness of a firm's EBIT to fluctuations in sales. Operating leverage results when fixed operating costs are present in the firm's cost structure. It should be noted here that fixed operating costs do *not* include interest charges incurred from the firm's use of debt financing.

B. Implications of operating leverage:

1. At each point above the break-even level, the degree of operating leverage decreases (i.e., the greater the sales level, the lower the DOL).

2. At the break-even level of sales, the degree of operating leverage is undefined.

3. Operating leverage is present anytime the percentage change in EBIT divided by the percentage change in sales is greater than one.

4. The degree of operating leverage can be attributed to the business risk that a firm faces.

IV.   Financial Leverage

    A.   Financial leverage, as defined earlier, is the practice of financing a portion of the firm's assets with securities bearing a fixed rate of return in hopes of increasing the ultimate return to the common stockholders. To see if financial leverage has been used to benefit the common shareholders, the discussion here will focus on the responsiveness of the company's earnings per share (EPS) to changes in its EBIT. It should be noted here that not all analysts rely exclusively on this type of relationship. In fact, the weakness of such an approach will be examined in the following chapter.

    B.   The firm is using financial leverage and is exposing its owners to financial risk when:

$$\frac{\% \text{ change in EPS}}{\% \text{ change in EBIT}} \text{ is greater than } 1.00.$$

V.   Combining Operating and Financial Leverage

    A.   Since changes in sales revenues cause greater changes in EBIT, and if the firm chooses to use financial leverage, changes in EBIT turn into larger variations in both EPS and EAC (earnings available to common shareholders). Then, combining operating and financial leverage causes rather large variations in EPS.

    B.   The combined effects of operating and financial leverage is reflected in the following ratio:

$$= \frac{\% \text{ change in EPS}}{\% \text{ change in sales}}.$$

If the DCL is equal to 5.0 times, then it is important to understand that a 1% change in sales will result in a 5% change in EPS.

    C.   Implications of combining operating and financial leverage:

        1.   The total risk exposure that the firm assumes can be managed by combining operating and financial leverage in different degrees.

        2.   Knowledge of the various leverage measures that have been examined here aids the financial officer in his or her determination of the proper level of overall risk that should be accepted.

VI.   Introduction to Financing Mix Determination

    A.   A distinction can be made between the terms **financial structure** and **capital structure.**

        1.   Financial structure is the mix of all items that appear on the right-hand side of the firm's balance sheet.

        2.   Capital structure is the mix of the long-term, sources of funds used by the firm.

        3.   In this chapter, we do *not* dwell on the question of dealing with an appropriate maturity composition of the firm's sources of funds. Our main focus is on capital structure management, (i.e., determining the proper proportions relative to the total in which the permanent forms of financing should be used).

    B.   The *objective* of capital structure management is to mix the permanent sources of funds in a manner that will maximize the company's common stock price. This will minimize the firm's composite cost of capital. This proper mix of funds sources is referred to as the **optimal capital structure.**

VII.   Capital Structure Theory

    A.   The cost of capital-capital structure argument may be characterized by this question:

        1.   Can the firm affect its overall cost of funds, either favorably or unfavorably, by varying the mixture of financing sources used?

    B.   The argument deals with the postulated effect of the use of financial leverage on the overall cost of capital of the company.

    C.   If the firm's cost of capital can be affected by the degree to which it uses financial leverage, then capital structure management is an important subset of business financial management.

VIII.   Capital Structure Theory: A Moderate Position

    A.   The moderate position on capital structure importance admits to the facts that (1) interest expense is tax-deductible in the world of corporate activity and (2) the probability of the firm's suffering bankruptcy costs is directly related to the company's use of financial leverage.

B.   When interest expense is tax-deductible, the *sum* of the cash flows that the firm could pay to *all* contributors of corporate capital (debt investors and equity investors) is affected by its financing mix. This is *not* the case when an environment of no corporate taxation is presumed.

1.   The amount of the **tax shield on interest** may be calculated as:

$$\text{Tax shield} \quad = \quad r_d(D)(T)$$

where r_d =   the interest rate paid on outstanding debt,

D   =   the principal amount of the debt,

T   =   the firm's tax rate.

2.   The moderate position holds that the tax shield must have value in the marketplace. After all, the government's take is decreased, and the investor's take is increased because of the deductibility of interest expense.

3.   Therefore, according to this position, financial leverage affects firm value, and it must also affect the cost of corporate capital.

C.   To use too much financial leverage, however, would be imprudent. It seems reasonable to offer that the probability that the firm will be unable to meet the financial obligations contained in its debt contracts will increase the more the firm uses leverage-inducing instruments (debt) in its capital structure. The likelihood of firm failure, then, carries with it certain costs (bankruptcy costs) that rise as leverage use increases. There will be some point at which the expected cost of default will be large enough to outweigh the tax-shield advantage of debt financing. At that point, the firm will turn to common equity financing.

D.   Figure 12.1 depicts the moderate view on capital structure importance. This view of the cost of capital-capital structure argument produces a saucer-shaped or U-shaped average cost of capital curve. In Figure 12.1, the firm's optimal range of financial leverage use lies between points A and B. It would be imprudent for the firm to use additional financial leverage beyond point B because (1) the average cost of capital would be higher than it has to be and (2) the firm's common stock price would be lower than it has to be. Therefore, we can say that point B represents the firm's **debt capacity.**

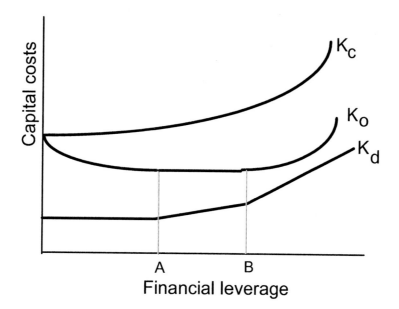

Figure 12.1
Capital Costs and Financial Leverage: The Moderate View That Considers Taxes and Financial Distress

E. We conclude that the determination of the firm's financing mix *is* centrally important to both the financial manager and the firm's owners.

IX. Firm Value and Agency Costs

A. Agency problem results in costs to the firm's owners to monitor management actions.

B. Capital structure management has given rise to agency costs associated with conflict between a firm's stockholders and bondholders.

1. Covenants in bond contracts may reduce potential conflicts.

2. Costs associated with protective covenants are borne by shareholders.

3. Monitoring costs rise as the firm's use of financial leverage increases.

4. With higher degrees of financial leverage, costs associate with financial distress increases.

C.   Market value of a levered firm is the sum of the market value of the unlevered firm plus the present value of tax shields less the present value of the financial distress costs and of agency costs.

D.   Agency costs, free cash flow, and capital structure

1.   Free cash flow's cash flow in excess of that required to fund all positive NPV projects.

2.   Substantial free cash flow can lead to managerial misbehavior and poor discounts associated with expenditures of the cash.

X.   Basic Tools of Capital Structure Management

A.   Recall that the use of financial leverage has two effects on the earnings stream flowing to the firm's common stockholders: (1) the added variability in the earnings per share (EPS) stream that accompanies the use of fixed-charge securities, and (2) the level of EPS at a given earnings before interest and taxes level (EBIT) associated with a specific capital structure. The first effect is quantified by the degree of financial leverage measure. The second effect is analyzed by means of what is generally referred to as *EBIT-EPS* analysis.

B.   The objective of EBIT-EPS analysis is to find the EBIT level that will equate EPS regardless of the financing plan chosen (from among two plans) by the financial manager.

1.   A graphic analysis or an algebraic analysis can be used.

2.   Study problems at the end of this chapter illustrate the nature of EBIT-EPS analysis.

3.   EBIT-EPS analysis considers only the level of the earnings stream and ignores the variability (riskiness) in it. In other words, this tool of capital structure management disregards the implicit costs of debt financing. Therefore, it must be used with caution and in conjunction with other basic tools of capital structure management.

C.   **Comparative leverage ratios** provide another tool of capital structure management. This involves the computation of various balance sheet leverage ratios and coverage ratios. Information for the latter comes essentially from the income statement. The ratios that would exist under alternative financing plans can then be computed and examined for their suitableness to management.

D.   The use of *industry norms* in conjunction with comparative leverage ratios can aid the financial manager in arriving at an appropriate financing mix. Industry norms can be thought of as standards for comparison. We recognize that industry groupings contain firms whose basic business risk may differ widely. Nevertheless, corporate financial analysts, investment bankers, commercial loan officers, and bond rating agencies rely on industry classes in order to compute such "normal" ratios. Since so many observers are interested in industry standards, the financial officer must be interested too.

XI.   A Glance at Actual Capital Structure Management

A.   The opinions and practices of financial executives reinforce the major topics covered in this chapter. Most senior financial officers, for example, *do* believe there is an optimum capital structure for the corporation.

B.   **Target debt ratios** are widely used by financial officers. Surveys indicate that the firm's actual target debt ratio is affected by several factors including (1) the firm's ability to adequately meet its financing charges, (2) maintaining a desired bond rating, (3) providing an adequate borrowing reserve, and (4) exploiting the perceived advantages of financial leverage. In practice, the firm's *own management group and staff of analysts* seem to be the most important influence on actually setting the target debt ratio.

C.   In this chapter, we defined **debt capacity** as the maximum proportion of debt that the firm can include in its capital structure and still maintain its lowest composite cost of capital. Executives operationalize this concept in different ways. The most popular approach is to define the firm's debt capacity as a target percent of total capitalization (i.e., total long-term debt divided by the sum of all long-term debt, preferred equity, and common equity).

D.   In the opinion of your authors, the single most important factor that should affect the firm's financing mix is the underlying nature of the business in which it operates. This also means the firm's **business risk** must be carefully assessed. This means the firm's capital structure cannot be properly designed without a thorough understanding of its commercial (business) strategy.

XII.   Multinational Firm: Business Risk and Global Sales

    A.   Business risk for multinational firm is directly affected by

        1.   sensitivity of the firm's product demand to general economic conditions.

        2.   degree of competition.

        3.   product diversification.

        4.   growth prospects.

        5.   global sales volume and productive output.

    B.   Multinational firm expansion into foreign markets increases the firm's business risk.

Study Problems

1.   Columbia Products will earn $231,000 next year after taxes. Sales for Columbia will be $4,400,000. The firm operates in modern facilities near Columbia, South Carolina. The firm specializes in the production of furniture for lawyers' offices, accountants' offices, and college dormitories. The average unit sells for $220 and has an associated variable cost per unit of $165. Columbia experiences a 30% tax rate.

    (a)   What will fixed costs (in total) be next year for Columbia?

    (b)   Calculate Columbia's break-even point both in units and dollars.

    (c)   Generate the analytical income statement at the break-even level of sales dollars.

SOLUTION

    (a)   All that we have to do here is use our knowledge of the break-even model *and* the analytical income statement model (both are discussed in detail in Chapter 12 of your text). The calculations follow.

$$\{(P \cdot Q) - [V \cdot Q + (F)]\}\ (1 - T) = \$231,000$$

$$\left\{4,400,000 - \left[\$1.65 \times \frac{\$4,400,000}{\$220}\right] + F\right\}(1 - T) = 231,000$$

$$[(\$4,400,000) - (\$3,300,000) - F]\ (\cdot 7) = \$231,000$$

$$(\$1,100,000 - F)\ (.7) = \$231,000$$

$$\$770,000 - .7F = \$231,000$$

$$.7F = \$539,000$$

$$F = \underline{\$770,000}$$

(b) $\quad Q_B \quad = \quad \dfrac{F}{P-V} = \dfrac{\$770,000}{\$55} = 14,000 \text{ units}$

$$S^* \quad = \quad \dfrac{F}{1-\dfrac{VC}{S}} = \dfrac{\$770,000}{1-.75} = \dfrac{\$770,000}{.25}$$

$$= \quad \$3,080,000$$

We have shown that the firm will break even (i.e., EBIT= 0) when it sells 14,000 units. With a selling price of $220 per unit, the break-even sales level is $3,080,000.

(c) The analytical income statement at the break-even level of sales would appear as follows:

Sales	$3,080,000
Variable costs	2,310,000
Revenue before fixed costs	$ 770,000
Fixed costs	770,000
EBIT	$ 0

2. Woody's Carry-Out Pizza expects to earn $16,000 next year before interest and taxes. Sales will be $130,000. The store is the only pizza parlor near Gardiner University's fraternity-row. The owner, Eric Nemeth, makes only one variety and size of pizza (the House Special), and it sells for $10. The variable cost per pizza is $6. Woody's Carry-Out Pizza experiences a 48% tax rate.

(a) What are the pizza parlor's fixed costs expected to be next year?

(b) Calculate the parlor's break-even point in units and dollars.

SOLUTION

(a) To compute fixed costs:

$S - (VC + FC) = EBIT$

$\$130,000/\$10 = 13,000$ units sold

$\$130,000 - [(13,000)(\$6) + FC] \quad = \$16,000$

$\$130,000 \; - \; \$78,000 \; - \; FC \quad = \$16,000$

$FC \quad = \$36,000$

(b)   First, the break-even point in units:

$$Q_B = \frac{F}{P-V} = \frac{\$36,000}{\$10-\$6} = 9,000 \text{ units.}$$

Then, the break-even point in dollars:

$$S^* = \frac{F}{1-VC/S} = \frac{\$36,000}{1-\dfrac{\$78,000}{\$130,000}} = \$90,000.$$

3.   The ESM Corporation projects that next year its fixed costs will total $120,000. Its only product sells for $17 per unit, of which $9 is a variable cost. The management of ESM is considering purchasing a new machine, which will lower the variable cost per unit to $7. The new machine, however, will add to fixed costs through an increase in depreciation expense.

(a)   How large can the addition to fixed costs be in order to keep the firm's break-even point in units produced and sold unchanged?

SOLUTION

(a)   Compute the present level of break-even output:

$$Q_B = \frac{F}{P-V}$$

$$= \frac{\$120,000}{8} = 15,000 \text{ units}$$

Compute the new level of fixed costs at the break-even output:

$$F + (7)(15,000) = (17)(15,000)$$

$$F + 105,000 = 255,000$$

$$F = \$150,000$$

Compute the addition to fixed costs:

$$\$150,000 - \$120,000 = \$30,000 \text{ addition}$$

4.   The Moose Hobby Company manufactures a full line of gold-plated model airplanes. The average selling price of a finished unit is $25. The associated variable cost is $15 per unit. Fixed costs for the company average $70,000 per year. What would be the company's profit or loss if production sold were 5,000 units? 7,000 units? 9,000 units?

SOLUTION

The company's profit or loss:

	@ 5,000 units	@ 7,000 units	@ 9,000 units
Sales (P X Q)	$125,000	$175,000	$225,000
– VC (VC/unit X Q)	75,000	105,000	135,000
– FC	70,000	70,000	70,000
Profit (loss)	($ 20,000)	-0-	$ 20,000

5.   An analytical income statement for the D. A. Bauer Corporation is shown below. It is based on an output level of 69,000 units.

Sales	$1,035,000
Variable costs	552,000
Revenue before fixed costs	$ 483,000
Fixed costs	183,000
EBIT	$ 300,000
Interest expense	80,000
Earnings before taxes	$ 220,000
Taxes	77,000
Net income	$ 143,000

(a)   Calculate net income for a 10% increase in sales where variable costs increase in proportion to sales.

(b)   What is the effect of the firm's operating leverage on the firm's EBIT?

(c)   What is the effect of the firm's financial leverage on net income?

(d)   What is the combined effect of operating and financial leverage on the firm?

SOLUTION

		+10%	% Change
Sales	$1,035,000	$1,138,500	10%
Variable costs	552,000	907,200	
Revenue before fixed costs	$ 483,000	$ 531,300	
Fixed costs	183,000	183,001	
EBIT	$ 300,000	348,299	16%
Interest expense	80,000	80,001	
Earnings before taxes	$ 220,000	$ 268,298	
Taxes	77,000	93,904	
Net income	$ 143,000	$ 174,394	22%

(a)   The 10% increase in sales increases firm net income from $143,000 to $174,394. Note that fixed costs and interest expense do not change and this fact is the source of operating and financial leverage.

(b)   The 10% increase in sales is magnified to a 16% increase in EBIT by the firm's use of operating leverage.

(c)   The firm's use of financial leverage made the 16% increase in EBIT into a 22% increase in net income.

(d)   Combined the effects of operating and financial leverage are to make the increase in net income 2.2 times larger than the percent change in sales.

6.   E. Wrok and Associates, Inc., are planning to open a small manufacturing corporation. The company will manufacture a full line of solar-energized home products. The investors of the company have proposed two financing plans. Plan I is an all common equity alternative. Under this plan, 200,000 common shares will be sold to net the firm $20 per share. Financial leverage is stipulated in Plan II, and 100,000 shares will be sold. A debt issue with a 30-year maturity period will be placed privately. The interest rate on the debt issue will be 18% while the principal borrowed will amount to $2,000,000. The corporate tax rate is 50%.

(a)   Find the EBIT indifference level associated with the two financing proposals.

(b)   Prepare an income statement that shows that EPS will be the same regardless of the plan chosen at the EBIT level found in part a.

(c)   If a detailed financial analysis projects that long-term EBIT will always be close to $1,000,000 annually, which plan would be chosen? Why?

SOLUTION

(a)   In the following equation, E = EBIT.

$$\frac{(E - \$0)(1 - 0.5) - 0}{200,000} = \frac{(E - \$360,000)(1 - 0.5) - 0}{100,000}$$

$$\frac{0.5E}{200,000} = \frac{0.5E - \$180,000}{100,000}$$

$$\$50,000E = 100,000E - \$36,000,000,000$$

$$E = \underline{\$720,000}$$

(b)

Income Statement

	With C/S Financing	Financing with C/S and Debt
EBIT	$720,000	$720,000
Less: Interest expense	0	360,000
Earnings before taxes	$720,000	$360,000
Less: Taxes @ 50%	360,000	180,000
Earnings available to common	$360,000	$180,000
C/S outstanding	200,000	100,000
EPS	$1.80	$1.80

(c)   Plan II, because at any level above the indifference point, the more heavily levered financing plan will generate a higher EPS.

7.   Albina's Ice Cream Factory's capital structure for the past year of operations is shown below.

First Mortgage bonds at 15%	$ 4,000,000
Debentures at 17%	3,500,000
Common stock (1,500,000 shares)	10,500,000
Retained earnings	2,000,000
Total	$20,000,000

The federal income tax rate is 50%. Albina's Ice Cream Factory, home-based in San Antonio, wants to raise an additional $1,500,000 to open new facilities in Houston and Dallas. The firm can accomplish this via two alternatives. That is, it can sell a new issue of 20-year debentures with 18% interest; alternatively, 30,000 new shares of common stock can be sold to the public to net the ice cream factory $50 per share. A recent study performed by an outside consulting organization projected Albina's Ice Cream's long-term EBIT level at approximately $13,575,000.

(a) Find the indifference level of EBIT (with regard to earnings per share) between the suggested financing plans.

(b) Which alternative do you recommend that Albina's Ice Cream Factory pursue?

SOLUTION

(a) In the following equations, E = EBIT

$$\frac{(E - \$1,195,000)(0.5)}{1,530,000} = \frac{(E - \$1,465,000)(0.5)}{1,500,000}$$

$$\frac{0.5E - \$597,500}{153} = \frac{0.5E - \$732,500}{150}$$

$$75E - \$89,625,000 = 76.5E - \$112,072,500$$

$$E = \underline{\$14,965,000} \text{ indifference level of EBIT}$$

(b) The consulting firm projected Albina's Ice Cream Factory's long-term EBIT at $13,575,000. Since this projected level of EBIT is less than the indifference level of $14,965,000, the earnings per share of the firm will be greater if the common stock is issued.

Self Test

TRUE-FALSE

_____ 1. Dispersion in operating income causes business risk.

_____ 2. Your firm adds a completely automated product line to its facilities. This will have no effect on the break-even point (in units of output).

_____ 3. Variable costs are fixed per unit of output but vary in total as output changes.

_____ 4. Your firm expects a 7% increase in sales for the next year. The degree of operating leverage will decrease for your firm.

_____ 5. When the firm uses more financial leverage, its stockholders expect a greater return.

_____ 6. The break-even model enables the financial officer to determine the quality of output that must be sold to cover all operating costs.

_____ 7. If EBIT were to remain constant while the firm incurred additional interest expense, the degree of financial leverage would increase.

_____ 8. The incurrence of fixed operating costs in the firm's income stream is referred to as financial leverage.

_____ 9. Break-even analysis is a long-run concept since all costs are variable in the long run.

_____ 10. Operating leverage is the responsiveness of the firm's EBIT to fluctuations in net income.

_____ 11. Earnings per share is the most appropriate criterion for all financing decisions.

_____ 12. The decision by the firm to use financial leverage magnifies its variation in earnings per share, compared to the use of no financial leverage.

_____ 13. Variable costs are fixed per unit of output.

_____ 14. Fixed costs per unit vary with units of output.

_____ 15. Combining operating and financial leverage magnifies variations in earnings per share in response to changes in sales.

_____ 16. A firm faces a greater chance of insolvency with an increase in the use of financial leverage (other factors held constant).

_____ 17. The decision to use debt or preferred stock in the financial structure of a corporation means that those who own the common shares are exposed to financial risk.

_____ 18. Semi-variable costs may be fixed over a range of output, then rise sharply as a higher output level is reached and remain fixed over this higher range of output.

_____ 19. Break-even analysis *must* include allowance for all non-cash expenses.

_____ 20. Financial risk is a direct result of the firm's investment decisions.

_____ 21. Financial leverage is a result of the financing of the firm's assets with securities bearing a fixed rate of return over a specific time period.

_____ 22. Firms can affect their total risk exposures by combining operating and financial leverage in different degrees.

_____ 23. The ratio of total variable costs to total sales is presumed constant in ordinary break-even analysis.

_____ 24. Capital structure is defined by the mix of all items that appear on the right-hand side of the firm's balance sheet.

_____ 25. The major influence on the maturity structure of the financing plan is the nature of the assets owned by the firm.

_____ 26. The optimal capital structure can be defined as the mix of permanent sources of funds that minimize the company's common stock price.

_____ 27. The EBIT-EPS analysis measures the variability (riskiness) of the earnings stream, thereby recognizing the implicit costs of debt financing.

_____ 28. The tax shield on interest represents additional cash flow to a firm's security holders resulting from tax savings on interest payments to the firm.

_____ 29. In computing the firm's tax bill, the interest expense is assumed not to be tax deductible.

_____ 30. Inputs to the coverage ratios generally come from the firm's balance sheet.

_____ 31. According to the moderate position of capital structure theory, financial leverage affects firm value but not the cost of corporate capital.

_____ 32. Above a critical level of EBIT, the firm's earnings per share will be lower if greater degrees of financial leverage are employed.

_____ 33. Industry norms, used with other tools of capital structure management, can be helpful in determining an appropriate financing mix.

_____ 34. In practice, as more financial leverage is used, it will increase the firm's value indefinitely and lower its cost of capital continuously.

_____ 35. The EBIT-EPS analysis chart tells us that EPS will be greater than zero, if the EBIT level just covers the plan's financing cost.

_____ 36. At a point below the EBIT indifference level, the financing plan involving less leverage will generate a higher EPS.

_____ 37. Capital structure is equal to the financial structure less current liabilities.

_____ 38. Debt capacity is the maximum proportion of debt that a company can include in its capital structure without affecting the cost of common equity.

_____ 39. Agency costs refer to those expenses paid to lawyers, accountants, etc. during bankruptcy proceedings.

_____ 40. Financial managers must frequently use coverage ratios to operationalize debt capacity concepts.

_____ 41. External economic factors are an important influence on determining a firm's target debt ratio, but firm-specific factors have to be considered as well.

_____ 42. The purpose of EBIT-EPS analysis is to determine the level of operating income at which EBIT equals EPS for a single financing plan.

MULTIPLE CHOICE

1. Which of the following is *not* a limitation of break-even analysis?

   a. The price of the product is assumed to be constant.
   b. In multiple product firms, the product mix is assumed to be constant.
   c. It provides a method for analyzing operating leverage.
   d. Variable costs per unit are assumed to be constant.

2. Which of the following is not generally considered a fixed cost?

   a depreciation
   b. rent
   c. electricity
   d. administrative salaries

3. At the break-even level of sales, the degree of operating leverage is

   a. zero.
   b. undefined.
   c. a positive number.
   d. Not enough information is given.

4. In the context of break-even point in sales dollars, if the variable cost per unit rises and if all other variables remain constant, the break-even level of sales will

   a. fall.
   b. rise.
   c. stay the same.
   d. either a or c.
   e. None of the above are true.

5. The firm is exposing itself to financial risk when its percent change in EPS divided by percent change in EBIT is

   a. less than 1.
   b. greater than 1.
   c. equal to 1.
   d. between 0 and 1.
   e. none of the above.

6.   A firm that incurs a low level of fixed operating costs might prudently use
      a.   a low degree of financial leverage.
      b.   a high degree of financial leverage.
      c.   a low degree of combined leverage.
      d.   none of the above.

7.   As the firm's sales revenue increases over time,

      a.   it can lessen its business risks.
      b.   it can lessen its operating leverage.
      c.   both a and b
      d.   all of the above
      e.   none of the above

8.   The practice of financing a portion of a firm's assets with securities bearing a fixed rate of return in hopes of increasing the ultimate return to shareholders refers to

      a.   operating leverage.
      b.   financial leverage.
      c.   break-even sales level.
      d.   all of the above.
      e.   none of the above.

9.   The selling price of a product is $25, and the unit variable cost is $17. If a firm's fixed costs are $20,000, what is the break-even level in units?

      a.   800 units
      b.   2,000 units
      c.   2,500 units
      d.   4,300 units
      e.   none of the above

10.   Business risk is the residual effect of

      a.   the company's cost structure.
      b.   product demand characteristics.
      c.   intra-industry competitive position.
      d.   all of the above.
      e.   none of the above.

11.   The break-even model assumes that if sales increase by 10%, variable costs

    a.   remain unchanged.
    b.   rise by 10%.
    c.   rise by 20%.
    d.   The break-even model makes no assumptions about variable costs and sales.
    e.   None of the above are true.

12.   The break-even level for the number of units sold is defined as

    a.   (unit sales price minus unit variable cost) divided by total fixed costs.
    b.   unit sales minus (unit variable costs divided by total fixed costs).
    c.   (total fixed costs divided by unit sales price) minus unit variable costs.
    d.   trial and error analysis.
    e.   All are acceptable techniques.

13.   As the quantity of product increases, the fixed cost per unit of output

    a.   increases.
    b.   decreases.
    c.   remains constant.
    d.   increases to a certain level and then decreases.
    e.   none of the above.

14.   Operating leverage can be attributed to _____ that a firm assumes.

    a.   the financial risk
    b.   the business risk
    c.   Both a and b are true.
    d.   None of the above are true.

15.   Break-even analysis and its assumptions can help the financial officer determine the

    a.   level of output that must be sold to recover all operating costs.
    b.   EBIT that will be achieved at various output levels.
    c.   Both a and b are true.
    d.   None of the above are true.

16.   The firm's capital structure consists of

    a.   long-term debt.
    b.   common equity.
    c.   preferred equity.
    d.   only b and c.
    e.   none of the above.

17.	A firm will turn to common equity financing when

    a.	the stock market is looking favorable.
    b.	the expected cost of default is greater than the tax advantage of debt financing.
    c.	it reaches optimal capital structure.
    d.	only a and b occur.
    e.	None of the above are true.

18.	The objective of capital structure management is to

    a.	minimize the composite cost of capital.
    b.	determine the optimal capital structure.
    c.	maximize the common stock price.
    d.	All of the above are true.
    e.	None of the above are true.

19.	The cost of debt financing is _____ by the effects of income taxes.

    a.	increased
    b.	decreased
    c.	not affected
    d.	either increased or decreased depending on the level of the tax rate
    e.	None of the above are true.

20.	Which of the following assumptions does capital structure theory not include?

    a.	Corporate income is not subject to any tax.
    b.	Transaction costs of selling securities are prevalent.
    c.	The expected values of all investors' forecasts of the future levels of EBIT for each firm are identical.
    d.	The capital structures consist only of stocks and bonds.
    e.	None of the above; they are all assumptions of capital structure theory.

21.	Which of the following is not a limitation of EBIT-EPS analysis?

    a.	It disregards the explicit cost of debt financing.
    b.	It ignores the level of the firm's earnings stream.
    c.	There are no limitations of the EBIT-EPS analysis.
    d.	None of the above; they are all limitations of EBIT-EPS analysis.

22. Which of the following is not true about capital structure theory (moderate position)?

    a. Firm's bankruptcy cost is related to its use of financial leverage.
    b. The sum of the cash flows that the firm could pay to all contributors of corporate capital is not affected by its financing mix.
    c. Financial leverage affects the firm's value.
    d. a and c
    e. none of the above

23. Which of the following is *not* a basic tool of capital structure management?

    a. EBIT-EPS analysis
    b. comparative leverage ratios
    c. use of industry norms
    d. none of the above.

23. Which of the following are ways of analyzing capital structure?

    a. EBIT-EPS analysis
    b. comparative leverage ratios
    c. analysis of cash flows
    d. a and b
    e. none of the above

25. The optimal capital structure refers to a capital structure that
    a. is comprised of 99.9% debt capital.
    b. will minimize the composite cost of a firm's capital for raising a given amount of funds.
    c. will minimize the firm's common stock price.
    d. None of the above are true.

26. The target debt ratio is affected by the firm's ability to

    a. adequately meet its financing charges.
    b. maintain a desired bond rating.
    c. provide an adequate borrowing reserve.
    d. exploit the perceived advantages of financial leverage.
    e. All of the above are true.

CHAPTER 13

Dividend Policy and Internal Financing

<u>Orientation</u>: In determining the firm's dividend policy, two issues are important: the dividend payout ratio and the stability of the dividend payment over time. In this regard, the financial manager should consider the investment opportunities available to the firm and any preference that the company's investors have for dividend income or capital gains. Also, stock dividends, stock splits, or stock repurchases can be used to supplement or replace cash dividends.

I. The Trade-offs in Setting a Firm's Dividend Policy

    A. If a company pays a large dividend, it will

        1. have a low retention of profits within the firm, and

        2. need to rely heavily on a new common stock issue for equity financing.

    B. If a company pays a small dividend, it will

        1. have a high retention of profits within the firm, and

        2. will not need to rely heavily on a new common stock issue for equity financing since the profits retained for reinvestment will provide the needed equity financing.

II. The importance of a firm's dividend policy depends on the impact of the dividend decision on the firm's stock price. That is, given a firm's capital budgeting and borrowing decisions, what is the impact of the firm's dividend policies on the stock price?

III.   Three Views about the Importance of a Firm's Dividend Policy.

A.   View 1: Dividends do not matter

1.   Assume that the dividend decision does not change the firm's capital budgeting and financing decisions.

2.   Assume perfect markets, which means:

a.   There are no brokerage commissions when investors buy and sell stocks.

b.   New securities can be issued without incurring any flotation cost.

c.   There is no income tax—personal or corporate.

d.   Information is free and equally available to all investors.

e.   There are no conflicts of interest between management and stockholders.

3.   Under the forgoing assumptions, it may be shown that the market price of a corporation's common stock is unchanged under different dividend policies. If the firm increases the dividend to its stockholders, it has to offset this increase by issuing new common stock in order to finance the available investment opportunities. If, on the other hand, the firm reduces its dividend payment, it has more funds available internally to finance future investment projects. In either policy, the present value of the resulting cash flows to be accrued to the current investors is independent of the dividend policy. By varying the dividend policy, only the *type* of return is affected (capital gains versus dividend income), not the *total* return.

B.   View 2: High dividends increase stock value

1.   Dividends are more predictable than capital gains because management can control dividends, while they cannot dictate the price of the stock. Thus, investors are less certain of receiving income from capital gains than from dividend income. The incremental risk associated with capital gains relative to dividend income should, therefore, cause us to use a higher required rate in discounting a dollar of capital gains than the rate used for

discounting a dollar of dividends. In so doing, we would give a higher value to the dividend income than we would the capital gains.

2.   Criticisms of view 2

    a.   Since the dividend policy has no impact on the volatility of the company's overall cash flows, it has no impact on the riskiness of the firm.

    b.   Increasing a firm's dividend does not reduce the basic riskiness of the stock; rather, if dividend payment requires management to issue new stock, it only transfers risk *and* ownership from the current owners to new owners.

C.   View 3: Low dividends increase value

Stocks that allow investors to defer taxes (low dividends–high capital gains) will possibly sell at a premium relative to stocks that require investors to pay taxes currently (high dividends–low capital gains). Only then will the two stocks provide comparable after tax returns, which suggests that a policy to pay low dividends will result in a higher stock price. That is, high dividends hurt investors, while low dividends–high retention help the firm's investors.

In 2003, Congress felt the need to change the tax code again as it pertained to both dividend income and capital gains income. On May 28, President Bush signed into law the "Jobs and Growth Tax Relief Reconciliation Act of 2003." Recall that part of the impetus for this Act was the recession that commenced in 2001 and the slow rate of payroll jobs creation that followed that recession.

In a nutshell, the 2003 Act lowered the top tax rate on dividend income to 15 percent from a previous top rate of 38.6 percent, and also lowered the top rate paid on realized long-term capital gains from a previous 20 percent to the same 15 percent. Thus, you can see that the so-called investment playing field was (mostly) leveled for dividend income relative to qualifying capital gains. In effect, a major portion, but not all, of the previous bias against paying cash dividends to investors was mitigated.

D.   Additional thoughts about the importance of a firm's dividend policy

1.   **Residual dividend theory:** Because of flotation costs incurred in issuing new stock, firms must issue a larger amount of securities in order to receive the amount of capital required for investments. As a result, new equity capital will be more expensive than capital raised through retained earnings. Therefore, financing investments internally (and decreasing dividends) instead of issuing new stock may be favored. This is embodied in the **residual dividend theory,** where a dividend would be paid only when any internally generated funds remain after financing the equity portion of the firm's investments.

2.   **The clientele effect:** If investors do have a preference between dividends and capital gains, we could expect them to seek out firms that have a dividend policy consistent with these preferences. They would in essence "sort themselves out" by buying stocks that satisfy their preferences for dividends and/or capital gains. In other words, there would be a "clientele effect," where firms draw a given clientele, given the stated dividend policy. However, unless there is a greater aggregate demand for a particular policy than is being satisfied in the market, dividend policy is still unimportant, in that one policy is as good as the other. The clientele effect tells us only to avoid making capricious changes in a company's dividend policy.

3.   **The information effect**

a.   We know from experience that a large, unexpected change in dividends can have significant impact on the stock price. Despite such "evidence," it is not unreasonable to hypothesize that dividend policy only appears to be important because we are not looking at the real cause and effect. It may be that investors use a change in dividend policy as a **signal** about the firm's "true" financial condition, especially its earning power.

b.   Some would argue that management frequently has inside information about the firm that it cannot make available to the investors. This difference in accessibility to information between management and investors, called **information asymmetry,** may result in a lower stock price than if we had conditions of certainty. In a risky marketplace, dividends become a means to minimize any "drag" on the stock price that might come from differences in the level of information available to managers and investors.

4.   **Agency costs:** Conflicts between management and stock-holders may exist, and the stock price of a company owned by investors who are separate from management may be less than the stock value of a closely-held firm. The difference in price is the cost of the conflict to the owners, which has come to be called **agency costs.** Owners may perceive a firm's dividend policy as a tool to minimize agency costs. Assuming the payment of a dividend requires management to issue stock to finance new investments, then new investors will be attracted to the company only if management provides convincing information that the capital will be used profitably. Thus, the payment of dividends indirectly results in a closer monitoring of management's investment activities. In this case, dividends may provide a meaningful contribution to the value of the firm.

5.   **Expectations theory:** As the time approaches for management to announce the amount of its next dividend, investors form expectations as to how much the dividend will be. When the actual dividend decision is announced, the investor compares the actual decision with the expected decision. If the amount of the dividend is as expected, even if it represents an increase from prior years, the market price of the stock will remain unchanged. However, if the dividend is higher or lower than expected, the investors will reassess their perceptions about the firm and the value of the stock.

E.   Empirical evidence regarding the importance of dividend policy

1.   Statistical tests: To test the relationship between dividend payments and security prices, we could compare a firm's dividend yield (dividend/stock price) and the stock's total return, asking, "Do stocks that pay high dividends provide higher or lower returns to the investors?" Such tests have been conducted using a variety of the most sophisticated statistical techniques available. Despite the use of these extremely powerful analytical tools involving intricate and complicated procedures, the results have been mixed.

However, over long periods of time, the results have given a slight advantage to the low-dividend stocks; that is, stocks that pay lower dividends appear to have higher prices. The findings are far from conclusive, owing to the relatively large standard errors of the estimates.

2. Reasons for inconclusive results from the statistical tests

   a. To be accurate, we would need to know the amount of dividends investors *expect* to receive. Since these expectations cannot be observed, we can use only historical data, which may or may not relate to expectations.

   b. Most empirical studies have assumed a linear relationship between dividend payments and stock prices. The actual relationship may be nonlinear, and possibly even contain discontinuities in the relationship.

3. Since our statistical prowess does not provide us any conclusive evidence, researchers have surveyed financial managers with respect to their perceptions of the dividend policy's relevance. In such surveys, the evidence favors, but not overwhelmingly, the relevance of dividend policy. For the most part, managers are divided between believing that dividends are important and having no opinion in the matter.

F. Conclusions about the importance of dividend policy

   1. As a firm's investment opportunities increase, the dividend payout ratio should decrease.

   2. The firm's dividend policy appears to be important; however, appearances may be deceptive. The real issue may be the firm's *expected* earnings power and the riskiness of these earnings.

   3. If dividends influence stock price, it probably comes from the investor's desire to minimize and/or defer taxes and from the role of dividends in minimizing agency costs.

   4. If the expectations theory has merit, which we believe it does, it behooves management to avoid surprising investors when it comes to the firm's dividend decision.

IV.   Dividend Policy Decisions

    A.   Other practical considerations

        1.   **Legal restrictions**

            a.   A corporation may not pay a dividend

                (1)   If the firm's liabilities exceed its assets.

                (2)   If the amount of the dividend exceeds the accumulated profits (retained earnings).

                (3)   If the dividend is being paid from capital invested in the firm.

            b.   Debt holders and preferred stockholders may impose restrictive provisions on management, such as common dividends not being paid from earnings prior to the payment of interest or preferred dividends.

        2.   **Liquidity position:** The amount of a firm's retained earnings and its cash position are seldom the same. Thus, the company must have adequate *cash* available as well as retained earnings to pay dividends.

        3.   **Absence or lack of other sources of financing:** All firms do not have equal access to the capital markets. Consequently, companies with limited financial resources may rely more heavily on internally generated funds.

        4.   **Earnings predictability:** A firm that has a stable earnings trend will generally pay a larger portion of its earnings in dividends. If earnings fluctuate significantly, a larger amount of the profits may be retained to ensure that enough money is available for investment projects when needed.

        5.   **Ownership control:** For many small firms, and certain large ones, maintaining the controlling vote is very important. These owners would prefer the use of debt and retained profits to finance new investments rather than issue new stock.

6. **Inflation:** Because of inflation, the cost of replacing equipment has increased substantially. Depreciation funds tend to become insufficient. Hence, greater profit retention may be required.

B. Alternative dividend policies

1. **Constant dividend payout ratio:** The percentage of earnings paid out in dividends is held constant. Therefore, the dollar amount of the dividend fluctuates from year to year.

2. **Stable dollar dividend per share:** A relatively stable dollar dividend is maintained. The dividend per share is increased or decreased only after careful investigation by the management.

3. **Small, regular dividend plus a year-end extra:** Extra dividend is paid out in prosperous years. Management's objective is to avoid the connotation of a permanent dividend increase.

C. Bases for stable dividends

1. Investors may use the dividend policy as a surrogate for information that is not easily accessible. The dividend policy may be useful in assessing the company's long-term earnings prospects.

2. Many investors rely on dividends to satisfy personal income need. If dividends fluctuate from year to year, investors may have to sell or buy stock to satisfy their current needs, thereby incurring expensive transaction costs.

3. Legal listings stipulate that certain types of financial institutions may invest only in companies that have a consistent dividend payment.

4. Conclusion: An investor who prefers stable dividends will assign a lower required rate of return (a higher P/E ratio) for a stock paying a stable dividend. This results in a higher market price for the stock.

D. Dividend policy and corporate strategy: Things will change—even dividend policy.

   1. The recessions of 1990 to 1991 and 2001 induced a large number of American corporations to revisit their broadest corporate strategies, including adjusted dividend policies.

   2. One firm that altered its dividend policy in response to new strategies was the W.R. Grace & Co., headquartered in Columbia, Maryland.

   3. Table 13-1 in the text reviews W.R. Grace's actual dividend policies from 1992 to 1996. The firm's payout ratio and the absolute amount of the cash dividend paid per share declined significantly over this period.

V. Dividend Payment Procedures

   A. Dividends are generally paid quarterly.

   B. The **declaration date** is the date on which the firm's board of directors announces the forthcoming dividends.

   C. The **date of record** designates when the stock transfer books are to be closed thus identifying who is entitled to the dividend.

   D. Brokerage firms terminate the right of ownership to the dividend two working days prior to the date of record. This date is called the **ex-dividend date**.

   E. Dividend checks are mailed on the **payment date.**

VI. Stock Dividends and Stock Splits

   A. Both a stock dividend and a stock split involve issuing new shares of stock to current stockholders.

   B. The investor's percentage ownership in the firm remains unchanged. The investor is neither better nor worse off than before the stock split/dividend.

   C. On an economic basis, there is no difference between a stock dividend and a stock split.

D. For accounting purposes, the stock split has been defined as a stock dividend exceeding 25%.

E. Accounting treatment

1. For a stock dividend, the dollar amount of the dividend is transferred from retained earnings to the capital accounts.

2. In the case of a split, the dollar amounts of the capital accounts do not change. Only the number of shares is increased, while the par value of each share is decreased proportionately.

F. Rationale for a stock dividend or split

1. The price of stock may not fall precisely in proportion to the share increase; thus, the stockholders' value is increased.

2. If a company is encountering cash problems, it can substitute a stock dividend for a cash dividend. Investors will probably look beyond the dividend to determine the underlying reasons for conserving cash.

VII. Stock Repurchases

A. The following benefits justify stock repurchases instead of dividend payment:

1. To provide an internal investment opportunity.

2. To modify the firm's capital structure.

3. To impact earnings per share, thus increasing stock price.

B. Share repurchase as a dividend decision

1. A firm may decide to repurchase its shares, increasing the earnings per share which should be reflected in a higher stock price.

2. The investor's choice

a. For tax purposes, the investor may prefer the firm to repurchase stock in lieu of a dividend. Dividends are taxed as ordinary income, whereas any price appreciation resulting from the stock repurchase would be taxed as a capital gain.

b.   The investor may still prefer dividend payment because

(1)   Dividends are viewed as more dependable than potential stock price appreciation resulting from stock repurchases.

(2)   The price the firm must pay for its stock may be too high.

(3)   Riskiness of the firm's capital structure may increase, lowering the P/E ratio, and thus, the stock price.

C.   Financing or investment decision

1.   A stock repurchase effectively increases the debt-equity ratio towards higher debt; thus, repurchase is viewed as a financing decision.

2.   Buying its own stock at depressed prices, a firm may consider the repurchase as an investment decision. However, this action is not a true investment opportunity, as the extreme result would mean the company would consume itself.

D.   The repurchase procedure

1.   A public announcement should be made detailing the amount, purpose, and procedure for the stock repurchase.

2.   Open market purchase—at the current market price

3.   Tender offer—more formal and at a specified price

4.   Negotiated basis—repurchasing from specific large shareholders

VIII.   Multinational Firm: Dividend Payments Versus Reinvesting in the Firm

A.   During economic expansion periods, firms tend to focus on growth strategies and invest more earnings into positive NPV projects rather than dividend payments.

B.   Multinational firms look to international markets for high NPV projects to

1.   spread country-related economic risks by geographically diversifying, and

2.   achieve cost advantage over competitors.

C.   U.S. multinational firms tend to

1.   invest in opportunities in the United Kingdom and Canada,

2.   concentrate investments in manufacturing industries.

Study Problems

1.   Philips Limited treats dividends as a residual variable in its financial decisions (see residual dividend theory). Net income has been forecasted for the upcoming year to be $600,000, which may be used for reinvesting in the firm or for paying dividends. The firm has only equity in its capital structure, and its cost of internally generated equity capital is 10%. If, however, new common stock were issued, flotation costs would raise this cost to 11%. If the firm considers the 10% cost of internal equity to be the opportunity cost of retained earnings,

(a)   (1)   How much in dividends should be paid if the company has $500,000 in projects with expected returns exceeding 10%?

(2)   How much should the dividend be if $600,000 in investments are available having expected returns greater than 10%?

(b)   How much should be paid in dividends if the firm has $1 million in projects whose expected returns exceed 11%?

(c)   How would your answer change in part (b) if the firm's optimal debt-equity mix is 40% debt and 60% common equity and the cost of capital remains the same?

SOLUTION

(a)   (1)   According to the residual dividend theory, the firm should pay dividends only when it has exhausted its investments whose returns exceed the firm's cost of capital. Therefore, the firm should pay $100,000 in dividends ($600,000 income available for investing less $500,000 investments).

(2)   The firm should use all of the $600,000 for investing in the projects and should not pay any dividends.

(b)   If the firm has investment opportunities with returns exceeding the cost of capital, the firm should undertake these investments. In this example, the cost of capital increases (to 11%) when new equity is issued. Since the returns on the available investment projects (totaling $1 million) exceed the cost of equity capital, the firm should use up its internally generated funds ($600,000) and raise the remaining $400,000 by issuing new common stock. Therefore, no dividends would be paid.

(c)   We would need $400,000 in new debt, (i.e., 40% of $1 million). The remaining $600,000 (which is 60% of the needed capital) will be supplied by internally generated funds. No dividend will be paid.

2.   Beardsell Products and Voltas Products are identical firms in terms of (1) being in the same industry, (2) producing the same products, (3) being subject to the same risks, and (4) having equivalent earnings per share. Beardsell pays a constant cash dividend, whereas Voltas follows a constant percentage payout ratio of 50%. However, Voltas' common stock price has been lower than Beardsell's in spite of Voltas' dividend being substantially larger than Beardsell's in certain years. Given the data below:

	Beardsell Products			Voltas Products		
Year	EPS	Dividend	Market Price	EPS	Dividend	Market Price
2007	$2.50	$0.65	9	$2.50	$1.25	6 ¾
2008	−0.25	0.65	8 ¾	-0.25	0	6 ½
2009	3.00	0.65	9 ¼	3.00	1.50	9
2010	2.00	0.65	9	2.00	1.00	10

(a)   What might account for the differences in the market prices of the two companies?

(b)   What might both companies do in order to enhance the market prices of their respective shares?

SOLUTION

(a)   The dissimilarity between market prices might be a function of the different dividend policies, with a lower capitalization rate, and, accordingly, a higher price being assigned to Beardsell as a result of the stable dividend stream.

(b)   It appears that neither company would appear to be growth oriented. If both firms are valued in terms of their dividend yield, which seems to be the case, higher dividend payouts might produce higher prices.

3. Rexall Corporation is considering five investment opportunities. The required investment outlays and expected rates of return for these investments are shown below. The cost of capital for the firm is 13%. Investments are to be financed with 30% debt and 70% equity. Internally generated funds available for reinvestment equal $1 million.

(a) Which investments should be accepted?

(b) According to the residual dividend theory, what amount should be paid out in dividends?

Investment	Cost	Internal Rate of Return
A	$200,000	20%
B	300,000	15
C	900,000	14
D	100,000	10
E	400,000	7

SOLUTION

(a) Investments A, B, and C should be accepted because their expected returns exceed the firm's cost of capital.

(b) Dividends to be paid:

Total cost of three projects:

$200,000 + $300,000 + $900,000	=	$1,400,000
Equity financing: $1,400,000 x 70%	=	980,000
Debt financing: $1,400,000 − $980,000	=	420,000

Internally generated funds available:	$1,000,000
Less equity necessary for projects:	980,000
Funds available for dividend payment:	$ 20,000

<u>Self Tests</u>

TRUE-FALSE

_____ 1. If dividend policy is treated as a passive residual, dividends are paid only if the firm has any remaining capital after financing attractive investments.

_____ 2. In practice, the firm should invest retained earnings as long as the required rate of return exceeds the expected rate of return from the investment.

_____ 3. The greater the ability of a firm to borrow, the less is its ability to pay a cash dividend.

_____ 4. If a firm has sporadic investment opportunities, it might be expected to pay out more dividends.

_____ 5. The introduction of flotation costs to the "dividend irrelevance" concept favors the retention of earnings in the firm.

_____ 6. Dividend income and capital gains from the sale of stock are taxed at the same personal income tax rate. Thus, capital gains have no advantage over dividend income for the investor.

_____ 7. An "expected" change in the dividend policy of a firm may not affect the price of the firm's stock when the change is actually announced.

_____ 8. Stock repurchases increase the debt-to-equity ratio.

_____ 9. Stock repurchases offer an attractive investment alternative for the firm any time its stock price is depressed.

_____ 10. The "bird-in-the-hand" theory assigns a higher value to capital gains than to dividend income.

_____ 11. A firm's dividend policy affects the variability of the firm's overall cash flows, even when we do not allow the dividend policy to impact investment decisions.

_____ 12. Stocks that allow us to defer taxes will not sell at a premium.

MULTIPLE CHOICE

1.   Which of the following is not an assumption of the "dividend irrelevance" theory?

   a.   no taxes
   b.   efficient capital markets
   c.   no flotation costs
   d.   costless information
   e.   none of the above.

2.   An argument for the relevance of dividends would be

   a.   informational content.
   b.   resolution of uncertainty.
   c.   preference for current income.
   d.   all of the above.
   e.   none of the above.

3.   An advantage of a stock dividend is that it

   a.   may help to conserve cash.
   b.   tends to increase the market price.
   c.   keeps the price of the stock within a desired trading range.
   d.   All of the above are advantages.
   e.   None of the above are advantages.

4.   When the assumption of no taxes is removed from the "dividend irrelevance" theory

   a.   there is a preference for the retention of earnings.
   b.   there is a preference for paying out dividends.
   c.   the preference depends on the individual investor's tax status, but generally there is a preference for retention of earnings.
   d.   All of the above are true.
   e.   None of the above are true.

5. Which of following factors may influence what dividend policy that a firm undertakes?

    a. the liquidity of the firm
    b. capital structure
    c. legal restrictions
    d. a and c
    e. a and b

6. An advantage of a stock repurchase may be

    a. a means to modify capital structure.
    b. to impact earnings per share.
    c. the elimination of a particular minority group.
    d. all of the above.
    e. none of the above.

7. A firm may not legally pay dividends if

    a. its liabilities exceed its assets.
    b. the dividend is being paid from capital invested in the firm.
    c. debt holders' contracts are not satisfied.
    d. All of the above are true.
    e. None of the above are true.

8. For tax purposes, a corporation may exclude _____ of the dividend income received from another corporation.

    a. 0%
    b. 10%
    c. 50%
    d. 70%
    e. none of the above

9. When real-world considerations are taken into account, the amount of a firm's dividend payment depends on which of the following factors?

    a. profitability of investment opportunities
    b. investor's preference for capital gains or dividend income
    c. debt-to-equity ratio
    d. all of the above
    e. both a and b

10. Small-sized firms generally use retained earnings for investment purposes because

    a. they do not have easy access to the capital markets.
    b. ownership control is an important factor.
    c. their earnings fluctuate widely.
    d. inflation has greater impact on small companies.
    e. Both a and b are true.

11. Which one of the following dividend policies is the most popular?

    a. constant dividend payout ratio
    b. stable dividend (dollar) per share
    c. small, regular dividend plus a year-end extra
    d. all of the above
    e. none of the above

12. The ex-dividend date is

    a. the same as the date of record.
    b. two working days prior to date of record.
    c. eight days prior to the payment date.
    d. five days after the declaration date.
    e. none of the above.

13. Properly viewed, a stock repurchase should be used as

    a. a dividend decision.
    b. an investment decision.
    c. a refinancing decision.
    d. both a and c.
    e. none of the above.

CHAPTER 14

Short-Term Financial Planning

<u>Orientation</u>: In this chapter, we develop predictions of the firm's future financing needs based on a sales forecast. This entails construction of a pro forma income statement and balance sheet. The chapter also reviews the preparation and use of the cash budget as an essential tool of financial planning.

I.   Financial Forecasting and Planning

    A.   The need for forecasting in financial management arises whenever the future financing needs of the firm are being estimated. There are three basic steps involved in predicting financing requirements.

        1.   Project the firm's sales revenues and expenses over the planning period.

        2.   Estimate the levels of investment in current and fixed assets, which are necessary to support the projected sales level.

        3.   Determine the financing needs of the firm throughout the planning period.

    B.   The key ingredient in the firm's planning process is the sales forecast. This forecast should reflect (1) any past trend in sales that is expected to continue and (2) the effects of any events, which are expected to have a material effect on the firm's sales during the forecast period.

    C.   The traditional problem faced in financial forecasting begins with the sales forecast and involves making forecasts of the impact of predicted sales on the firm's various expenses, assets, and liabilities. The technique we use to make these forecasts is the **percent of sales** method. This involves projecting the financial variable as a percent of projected sales.

II. Profitability, Dividend Policy, and Discretionary Financing Needs (DFN)

    A. A firm's Discretionary Financing Needs (DFN) is the amount of financing the firm needs to obtain from discretionary (non-spontaneous) sources in order to finance its assets.

    B. Spontaneous sources of financing include accounts payable and other liabilities (e.g., wages payable) that arise "spontaneously" as the firm conducts its business plus the firm's net income less any dividends it pays. Consequently, the firm's dividend policy has a direct impact on its sources of spontaneous financing and consequently the firm's needs for discretionary financing, (i.e., discretionary financing needs or DFN).

III. Revenue Growth and DFN

    A. Revenue growth has two effects on DFN. First, revenue growth requires the firm to invest in additional working capital (current assets less current liabilities). Furthermore, with growing revenues the firm's profits generally increase with the effect of increasing the availability of funds to be retained and reinvested in the business.

VI. Financial Planning and the Cash budget

    A. The cash budget represents a detailed plan of future cash flows and can be broken down into four components: cash receipts, cash disbursements, net change in cash for the period, and new financing needed.

    B. Although no strict rules exist, as a general rule, the budget period shall be long enough to show the effect of management policies, yet short enough so that estimates can be made with reasonable accuracy. For example, the capital expenditure budget may be properly developed for a 10-year period while a cash budget may cover only 12 months.

Study Problems

1. The most recent balance sheet for the Parino Manufacturing Co. is shown in the table below. The company is about to embark on an advertising campaign, which is expected to increase sales from the present level of $10 million to $12 million by the end of next year. The firm is presently operating at full capacity and will have to increase its investment in both current and fixed assets to support the projected level of new sales. In fact, the firm estimates that both categories of assets will rise in direct proportion to the projected increase in sales.

    The firm's net profits were 4% of current year's sales but are expected to rise to 5% of next year's sales. To help support its anticipated growth in asset needs next year, the firm has suspended plans to pay cash dividends to its stockholders. In past years, a $1.50 per share dividend has been paid annually.

    Parino Manufacturing Co., Inc. ($ millions)

	Present Level	Percent of Sales	Projected Level
Current assets	$2.0		
Net fixed assets	3.0		
Total	$5.0		
Accounts payable	$0.5		
Accrued expenses	0.5		
Notes payable	—		
Current liabilities	$1.0		
Long-term debt	$2.0		
Common stock	0.5		
Retained earnings	1.5		
Common equity	$2.0		
Total	$5.0		

    Parino's payables and accrued expenses are expected to vary directly with sales. In addition, notes payable will be used to supply the funds needed to finance next year's operations that are not forthcoming from other sources.

    Fill in the table and project the firm's needs for discretionary financing. Use notes payable as the balancing entry for future discretionary financing needed.

SOLUTION ($ millions)

Current sales	$10	
Predicted sales	12	
Net profit margin	5%	

	Present Level	Percent of Sales	Projected Level
Current assets	$2.00	0.20	$2.40
Net fixed assets	3.00	0.30	3.60
Total	5.00	0.50	6.00
Accounts payable	0.50	0.05	0.60
Accrued expenses	0.50	0.05	0.60
Notes payable	——		——
Current liabilities	1.00	0.10	1.20
Long-term debt	2.00	No Change	2.00
Common stock	0.50	No Change	0.50
Retained earnings	1.50	Ret. Earnings + NI	2.10
Common equity	2.00		2.60
Total	$5.00		
Total financing provided			$5.80
Discretionary financing needed			$ .20

2. The Horn Corporation's projected sales for the first eight months of 2011 are as follows:

January	$300,000	May	$1,200,000
February	450,000	June	1,000,000
March	540,000	July	900,000
April	960,000	August	700,000

Twenty percent of Horn's sales are for cash, another 40% is collected in the month following the sale, and 40% is collected in the second month following the sale. November and December sales for 2000 were $800,000 and $650,000, respectively.

Horn purchases raw materials equal to 60% of sales, and it makes its purchases two months in advance of sales. The supplier is paid one month after the purchase. For example, purchases for April sales are made in February and are paid for in March.

Furthermore, Horn pays $42,000 per month for rent and $90,000 per month for other expenditures. Finally, tax deposits of $85,000 are made each quarter, beginning in March.

The company's cash balance at December 31, 2010, was $80,000, and a minimum balance of $50,000 must be maintained at all times. Assume that any short-term financing needed to maintain the minimum cash balance would be paid off in the month following the month of financing with interest paid at a 12% annual rate.

Prepare a cash budget for Horn covering the first six months of 2011.

SOLUTION

	January	February	March	April	May	June	July
Sales	$300,000	$450,000	$540,000	$960,000	$1,200,000	$1,000,000	$ 900,000
Cash sales	60,000	90,000	108,000	192,000	240,000	200,000	180,000
Collections 1 month later	260,000	120,000	180,000	216,000	384,000	480,000	400,000
2 months later	320,000	260,000	120,000	180,000	216,000	384,000	480,000
Total collections from sales	640,000	470,000	408,000	588,000	840,000	1,064,000	1,060,000
Purchases	324,000	576,000	720,000	600,000	540,000	420,000	420,000
Payments on purchases	270,000	324,000	576,000	720,000	600,000	540,000	
Cash receipts:							
Collections from sales	640,000	470,000	408,000	588,000	840,000	1,064,000	1,060,000
Cash disbursements:							
Payments on purchases	270,000	324,000	576,000	720,000	600,000	540,000	420,000
Other expenditures	90,000	90,000	90,000	90,000	90,000	90,000	90,000
Rent	42,000	42,000	42,000	42,000	42,000	42,000	42,000
Tax deposits			85,000			85,000	
Total disbursements	402,000	456,000	793,000	852,000	732,000	757,000	552,000
Net change for the month	238,000	14,000	(385,000)	(264,000)	108,000	307,000	
Beginning cash balance	80,000	318,000	332,000	50,000	50,000	50,000	
Plus: net change	238,000	14,000	(385,000)	(264,000)	108,000	307,000	
Borrowing (repayment)	-----	-----	103,000	265,000	(104,320)	(263,710)	
Interest for prior month's borrowing	-----	-----	-----	1,030*	3,680	2,637	
Ending cash balance	$318,000	$332,000	$ 50,000	$ 50,000	$ 50,000	$ 90,653	
Cumulative borrowing	-----	-----	-----	$368,030	$263,710		

*0.12 x 103,000 x 1/12 = $1,030

186
©2011 Pearson Education, Inc. Publishing as Prentice Hall

<u>Self Tests</u>

TRUE-FALSE

_____ 1. Budgets perform the basic functions of (1) providing the basis for taking corrective action and (2) providing the basis for performance evaluation.

_____ 2. DFN is the acronym for Discretionary Financing Needs.

_____ 3. Depreciation expense is an essential element in the cash budget.

_____ 4. Performance evaluation is an important function that can be performed through the use of budgets.

_____ 5. Research and development expenditures do not impact a firm's cash budget.

_____ 6. Discretionary financing needs are defined by the rate at which a firm's sales and the availability of non-discretionary sources of financing.

_____ 7. The budget planning period should never exceed six-months so that estimates can be made with reasonable accuracy.

_____ 8. The plowback or retention ratio reflects the proportion of a firm's earnings that are paid in dividends.

_____ 9. The cash budget is only as useful as the accuracy of the forecasts that are used in its preparation.

_____ 10. Depreciation expense reduces a firm's cash flow for the year in which the expense is recognized and incorporated in the firm's income statement.

MULTIPLE CHOICE

1. The most important element in determining the accuracy of most cash budgets is

    a. the forecast of cash disbursements.
    b. the forecast of the firm's collection schedule for accounts receivable.
    c. the forecast of sales.
    d. It cannot be determined.
    e. none of the above.

2. The cash budget embodies

    a. forecasts of prospective future cash balances of the firm.
    b. forecasts of actual cash expenditures and receipts.
    c. forecasts of the firm's personnel requirements.
    d. all of the above.
    e. a and b only.

3. Which of the following items would be included in the cash budget?

    a. depreciation charges
    b. goodwill
    c. patent amortization
    d. all of the above
    e. none of the above

4. Which of the following is provided by the cash budget?

    a. the exact amount of borrowing needed for the budget interval
    b. the type of loan that should be obtained to meet the cash needs for the time interval
    c. a point estimate of the borrowing needs for the budget interval
    d. an estimate of the cash needed for depreciation expense
    e. none of the above

5. Spontaneous sources of financing include which of the following?

    a. wages payable
    b. taxes payable
    c. short-term bank loans
    d. commercial paper
    e. a and b only

CHAPTER 15

Working-Capital Management

Orientation: In this chapter, we introduce working-capital management in terms of managing the firm's liquidity. Specifically, net working capital is defined as the difference in current assets and current liabilities. The hedging principle is offered as one approach to addressing the firm's liquidity problems. In this chapter, we also discuss sources of short-term financing that must be repaid within one year.

I.   Managing Current Assets

    A.   The firm's investment in current assets (such as fixed assets) is determined by the marginal benefits derived from investing in them compared with their acquisition cost.

    B.   However, the current fixed-asset mix of the firm's investment in assets is an important determinant of the firm's liquidity. That is, the greater the firm's investment in current assets, other things remaining the same, the greater the firm's liquidity. This is generally true since current assets are usually more easily converted into cash.

    C.   The firm can invest in marketable securities to increase its liquidity. However, such a policy involves committing the firm's funds to a relatively low-yielding (in comparison to fixed assets) investment.

II. Managing the Firm's Use of Current Liabilities

    A.   The greater the firm's use of current liabilities, other things being the same, the less will be the firm's liquidity.

    B.   There are a number of **advantages** associated with the use of current liabilities for financing the firm's asset investments.

        1.   **Flexibility.** Current liabilities can be used to match the timing of a firm's short-term financing needs exactly.

2. **Interest cost.** Historically, the interest cost on short-term debt has been lower than that on long-term debt.

C. Following are the **disadvantages** commonly associated with the use of short-term debt:

1. Short-term debt exposes the firm to an increased **risk of illiquidity** because by definition, short-term debt matures sooner and in greater frequency than does long-term debt.

2. Because short-term debt agreements must be renegotiated from year to year, the **interest cost** of each year's financing **is uncertain.**

III. Determining the Appropriate Level of Working Capital

A. Pragmatically, it is impossible to derive the "optimal" level of working capital for the firm. Such a derivation would require estimation of the potential costs of illiquidity which, to date, have eluded precise measurement.

B. However, the "hedging principle" provides the basis for the firm's working-capital decisions.

1. The **hedging principle** or **rule of self-liquidating debt** involves the following: The asset needs of the firm not financed by spontaneous sources (i.e., payables and accruals) should be financed in accordance with the following rule: Permanent asset investments are financed with permanent sources and temporary investments are financed with temporary sources of financing.

2. A **permanent investment in an asset** is one which the firm expects to hold for a period longer than one year. Such an investment may involve current or fixed assets.

3. **Temporary asset investments** comprise the firm's investment in current assets that will be liquidated and *not* replaced during the year.

4. **Spontaneous sources of financing** include all those sources that are available upon demand (e.g., trade credit—accounts payable) or that arise naturally as a part of doing business (e.g., wages payable, interest payable, taxes payable, etc.).

5. **Temporary sources of financing** include all forms of current or short-term financing not categorized as spontaneous. Examples include bank loans, commercial paper, and finance company loans.

6. **Permanent sources of financing** include all long-term sources such as debt having a maturity longer than one year, preferred stock, and common stock.

C. Although the hedging principle provides a useful guide to the firm's working-capital decisions, no firm will follow its tenets strictly. At times, a firm may rely too much on temporary financing for its cash needs, or it may have excess cash as a result of excessive use of permanent financing.

IV. Determining the Appropriate Level of Short-term Financing

A. The hedging concept was presented as one basis for determining the firm's use of short-term debt.

B. Hedging involves attempting to match temporary needs for funds with short-term sources of financing and permanent needs with long-term sources.

V. Selecting a Source of Short-term Financing

A. In general, three basic factors should be considered in selecting a source of short-term financing.

1. The effective cost of the credit source

2. The availability of credit

3. The effect of a particular source of credit on the cost and availability of other sources

B. The basic procedure used in estimating the cost of short-term credit utilizes the basic interest equation, (i.e., interest = principal x rate x time).

C. The problem in assessing the cost of a source of short-term financing involves estimating the annual percentage rate (APR) where the interest amount, the principal sum, and the time for which financing will be needed is known. Thus, the basic interest equation is "rearranged" as follows:

$$\text{APR} = \frac{\text{interest}}{\text{principal}} \; \text{x} \; \frac{1}{\text{time}}.$$

D. Compound interest was not considered in the simple APR calculation. To consider compounding, the following relation is used:

$$EAR = \left(1 + \frac{i}{M}\right)^M - 1$$

where EAR is the **effective annual rate**, i is the nominal rate of interest per year, and M is the number of compounding periods within one year. The effect of compounding is thus to raise the effective cost of short-term credit.

VI. Sources of Short-term Credit

A. The two basic sources of short-term credit are unsecured and secured credit.

1. Unsecured credit consists of all those sources where the only security is the lender's faith in the ability of the borrower to repay the funds when due.

2. Secured funds include additional security in the form of assets that are pledged as collateral in the event the borrower defaults in payment of principal or interest.

B. There are three major sources of unsecured short-term credit: trade credit, unsecured bank loans, and commercial paper.

1. Trade credit provides one of the most flexible sources of financing available to the firm. To arrange for credit, the firm need only place an order with one of its suppliers. The supplier then checks the firm's credit and if the credit is good, the supplier sends the merchandise.

2. Commercial banks provide unsecured short-term credit in two basic forms: lines of credit and transaction loans (notes payable). Maturities of both types of loans are usually one year or less with rates of interest depending on the credit-worthiness of the borrower and the level of interest rates in the economy as a whole.

3. A line of credit is generally an informal agreement or understanding between the borrower and the bank as to the maximum amount of credit that the bank will provide the borrower at any one time. There is no "legal" commitment on the part of the bank to provide the stated credit. There is another variant of this

form of financing referred to as a **revolving credit agreement** whereby such a legal obligation is involved. The line of credit generally covers a period of one year corresponding to the borrower's "fiscal" year.

4. Transaction loans are another form of unsecured short-term bank credit. The transaction loan, in contrast to a line of credit, is made for a specific purpose.

5. Only the largest and most creditworthy companies are able to use commercial paper, which consists of unsecured promissory notes in the money market.

   a. The maturities of commercial paper are generally six months or less with the interest rate slightly lower than the prime rate on commercial bank loans. The new issues of commercial paper are either directly placed or dealer placed.

   b. A number of advantages accrue to users of commercial paper: interest rates are generally lower than rates on bank loans and comparable sources of short-term financing; no minimum balance requirements are associated with commercial paper; and commercial paper offers a firm with very large credit needs a single source for all its short-term financing. Since it is widely recognized that only the most creditworthy borrowers have access to the commercial paper market, its use signifies a firm's credit status.

   c. However, a very important "risk" is involved in using this source of short-term financing; the commercial paper market is highly impersonal and denies even the most creditworthy borrower any flexibility in terms of repayment.

C. Secured sources of short-term credit have certain assets of the firm, such as accounts receivable or inventories, pledged as collateral to secure a loan. Upon default of the loan agreement, the lender has first claim to the pledged assets.

   1. Generally, a firm's receivables are among its most liquid assets. Two secured loan arrangements are generally made with accounts receivable as collateral.

a. Under a **pledged accounts receivable** arrangement, the amount of the loan is stated as a percentage of the face value of the receivables pledged.

b. **Factoring accounts receivable** involves the outright sale of a firm's accounts receivables to a factor.

2. Four secured loan arrangements are generally made with inventory as collateral.

a. Under the **floating lien agreement,** the borrower gives the lender a lien against all the borrower's inventory.

b. The **chattel mortgage agreement** involves having specific items of inventory identified in the security agreement.

c. The **field warehouse financing agreement** means that the inventories used as collateral are physically separated from the firm's other inventories and are placed under the control of a third-party field warehousing firm.

d. **Terminal warehouse agreements** involve transporting the inventories pledged as collateral to a public warehouse that is physically removed from the borrower's premises.

Study Problems

1. In order to meet a temporary need for working capital during an upcoming seasonal peak in sales, Gregory Sales Co. needs $500,000. Gregory's bank has agreed to lend the funds for the necessary three-month interval at a rate of 12% with a 20% compensating balance. Gregory Sales Co. normally maintains a demand deposit amount of $20,000. Estimate the annual (effective) cost of the loan to Gregory.

SOLUTION

To obtain the needed $500,000 and meet the compensating balance requirement, Gregory must borrow X dollars, where X is found as follows:

$$X - [0.20X - 20,000] = 500,000$$
$$0.80X = 480,000$$
$$X = \$600,000$$

Thus, Gregory borrows $600,000 for which it must maintain a compensating balance of 0.20 x 600,000 = $120,000, of which $20,000 will come from its normal demand deposit and $100,000 must be borrowed. This will leave the firm with the use of $500,000. The interest cost of the loan is computed as follows:

$$\text{Interest} = 0.12 \ \text{x} \ 600,000 \div 4 = \$18,000$$

We divide by 4 since the loan is for only three months or one-fourth of a year. The <u>effective</u> annual cost of the loan is:

$$\text{Rate} = \frac{\$\,\text{loan cost}}{\$\,\text{funds available}} \times \begin{array}{l}\text{loan maturity as a}\\\text{fraction of 1 year}\end{array}$$

$$= \frac{18,000}{500,000} \times \frac{1}{90/360} = \underline{0.144 \ \text{or} \ 14.44\%}$$

2.   A factor has agreed to buy Thomas Brothers' receivables ($250,000 per month), which have an average collection period of 90 days. The factor will advance up to 80% of the face value of the receivables for an annual charge of 10% of the funds advanced. The factor also charges a handling fee of 5% of the face value of all accounts purchased. What is the effective annual cost of the factoring arrangement to Thomas Brothers if the maximum advance is taken every month?

SOLUTION

With an average collection period of 90 days and monthly credit sales, Thomas Brothers could build up a loan advance over three months of 0.80 x 750,000 = $600,000. This loan would be constantly rolling over as accounts were being collected and as new credit sales were being made. The 90-day interest cost of the loan would be computed:

$$\text{Interest} = \$600,000 \ \text{x} \ \frac{0.10}{4} = \$15,000.$$

The factor's fee is calculated as follows:

$$\text{Fee} = 0.05 \ \text{x} \ \$750,000 = \$37,500.$$

Thus, the effective annual cost of the 90-day loan would be:

$$\text{Rate} = \frac{\$15,000 + \$37,500}{\$600,000} \div \frac{3}{12}$$

$$= \underline{0.35} \text{ or } \underline{35\%}$$

3. For the past seven years Warden Company has been factoring its accounts receivables. The factor's fee is 3%, and the factor will lend up to 90% of the volume of receivables purchased for an additional 1% per month. The firm typically has sales of $200,000 per month; 75% are on credit. Warden Company will save credit department costs of $3,500, since it will no longer need to operate a credit department. In addition, there will no longer be bad-debt losses, which previously were 1.25% per month.

The firm's bank has recently offered to lend the firm up to 90% of the face value of the receivables shown on the schedule of accounts. The bank would charge 9% per annum interest plus a 2% processing charge per dollar of receivables pledged. The firm extends terms of net 30, and all customers who plan to pay will do so by the thirtieth of the month. Should the firm discontinue its factoring arrangement in favor of the bank's offer if the firm borrows, on the average, $100,000 per month on its receivables?

SOLUTION

Factoring
The cost of factoring is:
Fee (0.03 x $200,000 x .75) $4,500
Interest cost (0.01 x $100,000)   1,000
                                                     $5,500 per month

Bank loan
The cost of the bank loan is:
Fee (0.02 x $100,000/.90) $2,222
Interest (0.09 x $200,000 x 1/12)   750
                                                     $2,972

Plus:
Credit department cost per month $2,500
Bad-debt losses ($200,000 x .75 x 0.0125)   1,875
  Total cost $7,375 per month

No, in this case, factoring is much cheaper. Note that we assume that the factor will absorb all credit risks and perform all credit functions saving the firm $2,500 + 1,875 = $4,375 per month.

4.   Calculate the effective cost of the following trade credit terms where payment is made on the net due date.

  (a)   2/10, net 30
  (b)   3/15, net 30
  (c)   3/15, net 45
  (d)   2/15, net 60

SOLUTION

  (a) $\dfrac{0.02}{0.98} \times \dfrac{1}{20/360} = 0.36734$ or 36.73%

  (b) $\dfrac{0.03}{0.97} \times \dfrac{1}{15/360} = 0.74226$ or 74.23%

  (c) $\dfrac{0.03}{0.97} \times \dfrac{1}{30/360} = 0.37113$ or 37.11%

  (d) $\dfrac{0.02}{0.98} \times \dfrac{1}{45/360} = 0.16327$ or 16.33%

5.   Luft, Inc., recently acquired production rights to an innovative sailboard design but needs funds to pay for the first production run, which is expected to sell briskly. The firm plans to issue $450,000 in 180-day maturity notes. The paper will carry an 11% rate with discounted interest and will cost Luft $13,000 (paid in advance) to issue.

  (a)   What is the effective cost of credit to Luft?

  (b)   What other factors should the company consider in analyzing whether to issue the commercial paper?

SOLUTION

  (a)   RATE $= \dfrac{\text{interest}}{\text{principal}} \times \dfrac{1}{\text{time}}$

$$\text{RATE} \quad = \quad \frac{\$24{,}750 * + 13{,}000}{\$450{,}000 - 13{,}000 - 24{,}750} \quad \text{X} \quad \frac{1}{180/360}$$

$$= \quad .1831 \text{ or } 18.31\%$$

$$*\text{Interest} \quad = \quad .11 \text{ x } \$450{,}000 \text{ x } \tfrac{1}{2}$$

(b)   The risk involved with issuing commercial paper should be considered. This risk relates to the fact that the commercial paper market is highly impersonal and denies even the most creditworthy borrower any flexibility in terms of when repayment is made. In addition, commercial paper is a viable source of credit to only the most creditworthy borrowers. Thus, it may simply not be available to the firm.

6.   DST, Inc., a producer of inflatable river rafts, needs $400,000 for the three-month summer season, ending September 30, 2001. The firm has explored two possible sources of credit.

(a)   DST has arranged with its bank for a $400,000 loan secured by accounts receivable. The bank has agreed to advance DST 80% of the value of its pledged receivables at a rate of 11% plus a 1% fee based on all receivables pledged. DST's receivables average a total of $1 million year-round.

(b)   An insurance company has agreed to lend the $400,000 at a rate of 9% per annum, using a loan secured by DST's inventory. A field warehouse agreement would be used, which would cost DST $2,000 a month.

Which source of credit should DST select? Explain.

SOLUTION

Pledged Receivables (A/R):

0.80 A/R	= $400,000 loan
A/R	= $400,000/.80 = $500,000
Fee	= (0.01) ($500,000) = $5,000
Interest cost	= (0.11) ($400,000) x ¼ = $11,000

$$\text{Effective rate} \quad = \quad \left(\frac{\$11{,}000 + 5{,}000}{\$400{,}000} \right) \left(\frac{1}{90/360} \right) = .16 \text{ or } 16\%$$

Inventory loan:

$$\text{Warehousing cost} = \$2{,}000 \times 3 \text{ months} = \$6{,}000$$

$$\text{Interest cost} = 0.09 \times \$400{,}000 \times \tfrac{1}{4} = \$9{,}000$$

$$\text{Effective rate} = \left(\frac{\$6{,}000 + 9{,}000}{\$400{,}000}\right)\left(\frac{1}{90/360}\right) = .15 \text{ or } 15\%$$

The inventory loan would be preferred since its cost is lowest under the conditions presented.

Self Tests

TRUE-FALSE

_____ 1. Working capital has traditionally been defined as the sum of the firm's investment in assets (both current and long-term assets).

_____ 2. Generally, interest rates on short-term debt are higher than they are on long-term debt for any given borrower.

_____ 3. The guiding principle for the firm's working capital policies is referred to as the "rule of self-liquidating debt" or the "hedging principle."

_____ 4. The use of short-term sources of financing generally enhances the firm's liquidity and reduces the firm's rate of return on assets.

_____ 5. There are two basic problems encountered in attempting to manage the firm's use of short-term financing: determining how much short-term debt to use and determining what sources to select.

_____ 6. Investment decisions are undertaken in the expectation of receiving future benefits.

_____ 7. In order to reduce its risk of illiquidity, a firm should decrease its investment in cash and marketable securities.

_____ 8. Current liabilities generally provide a more flexible source of financing than long-term debt.

_____ 9. The "hedging principle" is grounded in valuation theory.

_____ 10. Spontaneous financing consists of trade credit and other accounts payable which arise "automatically" in the firm's day-to-day operations.

_____ 11. The amount of trade credit available to the firm varies inversely with the size of the cash discount.

_____ 12. Compensating balances are never required when a firm has a line of credit with its bank.

_____ 13. A transaction loan is made for a specific purpose in mind for the funds involved.

_____ 14. An advantage of commercial paper to a creditworthy borrower is that repayment can be postponed if the firm finds itself in a liquidity squeeze.

_____ 15. Pledging involves selling accounts receivable to a financial intermediary known as a "factor."

_____ 16. The primary sources of collateral for secured short-term credit are accounts receivable and inventories.

_____ 17. Field warehouse financing agreements involve physically moving the pledged inventories to a public warehouse.

_____ 18. Commercial paper and trade credit are both forms of secured credit.

_____ 19. An advantage of trade credit is that the amount of credit extended expands and contracts with the needs of the firm.

MULTIPLE CHOICE

1. Which of the following is an advantage associated with the use of current versus long-term liabilities?

 a. The use of current liabilities subjects the firm to greater risk of illiquidity.
 b. The firm's interest costs can vary from year to year.
 c. The interest cost of current liabilities is generally higher than long-term debt.
 d. all of the above
 e. none of the above

2.   Spontaneous financing consists of

      a.   accounts payable.
      b.   trade credit.
      c.   short-term notes payable.
      d.   All of the above.
      e.   a and b only.

3.   Which of the following accounts would *not* be a prime consideration in working-capital management?

      a.   cash
      b.   accounts payable
      c.   corporate bonds
      d.   marketable securities
      e.   accounts receivable

4.   The greatest increase in margin of safety (liquidity) for a firm would be provided by

      a.   more current assets and less current liabilities.
      b.   more current assets and more current liabilities.
      c.   less current assets and more current liabilities.
      d.   less current assets and less current liabilities.
      e.   none of the above.

5.   Which asset-liability combination would result in the firm having the greatest risk of not being able to pay its bills on time?

      a.   more current assets and less current liabilities
      b.   more current assets and more current liabilities
      c.   less current assets and more current liabilities
      d.   less current assets and less current liabilities
      e.   none of the above

6.   Which of the following illustrates the use of the hedging approach?

      a.   temporary assets financed with long-term liabilities
      b.   permanent assets financed with long-term liabilities
      c.   temporary assets financed with short-term liabilities
      d.   all of the above
      e.   b and c

7.   Which of the following is not a form of secured short-term credit?

    a.   general lien
    b.   chattel mortgages
    c.   commercial paper
    d.   terminal warehouse receipt
    e.   factoring

8.   Under which of the following agreements does the borrower retain physical possession of the inventory used as collateral for a loan?

    a.   field warehouse financing
    b.   chattel mortgage
    c.   terminal warehouse
    d.   all of the above.
    e.   none of the above.

9.   An informal agreement between a bank and its customer with respect to the maximum amount of unsecured credit the bank will permit the firm to owe at any one time is

    a.   a line of credit agreement.
    b.   a revolving credit agreement.
    c.   a transaction loan.
    d.   none of the above.
    e.   all of the above.

10.   When a firm needs short-term funds for only one purpose, it usually obtains

    a.   a line of credit.
    b.   a revolving credit agreement.
    c.   a transaction loan.
    d.   a compensating balance.
    e.   none of the above.

CHAPTER 16

Current Asset Management

<u>Orientation</u>: This chapter initiates our study of liquidity management. Here, we focus on the cash flow process and the reasons why a firm holds cash balances. The objectives of a sound cash management system are identified. The concept of float is defined. Several techniques that firms can use to favorably affect their cash receipts and disbursement patterns are examined. Finally, the composition of the firm's marketable securities portfolio is discussed.

Additionally, the risk-return trade-off associated with the firm's investment in accounts receivable is discussed. For accounts receivable, this trade-off occurs as less creditworthy customers with a higher probability of bad debts are taken on to increase sales. The analysis is similar for sound inventory management. Here, a larger investment in inventory leads to more efficient production and speedier delivery; this should result in increased sales. However, additional financing costs to support the increase in inventory and increased handling and carrying costs are required.

I.   Why a Company Holds Cash

    A.   The firm's cash balance is constantly affected by a variety of influences. Sound cash management techniques are based on a thorough understanding of the cash flow process.

        1.   On an irregular basis, cash holdings are increased from several external sources, such as from the sale of securities.

        2.   In a similar fashion, irregular cash outflows reduce the firm's cash balance. Typical examples include cash dividend payments and the interest requirements on debt agreements.

        3.   Other major sources of cash arising from internal operations occur on a regular basis. Accounts receivable collections are an example.

B.   Three motives for holding cash balances have been identified by Keynes.[1]

1.   The **transactions motive** is the need for cash to meet payments that arise in the ordinary course of doing business. Holding cash to meet a payroll or to acquire raw materials characterizes this motive.

2.   The **precautionary motive** describes the investment in liquid assets that are used to satisfy possible but as yet indefinite needs for cash. Precautionary balances are a buffer against all kinds of things that might happen to drain the firm's cash resources.

3.   The **speculative motive** describes holding cash to take advantage of hoped-for, profit-making situations.

II.   Variations in Liquid Asset Holdings

A.   Considerable variation is present in the liquid asset holdings of major industry groups and individual firms.

1.   This is because (1) not all of the factors noted above affect every firm and (2) the executives in different firms who are ultimately responsible for cash management tasks have different risk-bearing preferences.

2.   Some industries invest heavily in liquid assets. For example, the total-liquid-assets-to-total-assets ratio of the contract construction industry greatly exceeds that of the utility industry.

B.   Because assets are acquired, used, and sold every day, the management of liquid assets must be viewed as a dynamic process. The cash flow process is complex. In order to cut through this complexity, it is necessary that the firm's cash management system operate within clearly defined objectives.

III.   Cash Management Objectives and Decisions

A.   A properly designed cash management program forces the financial manager to come to grips with a risk-return trade-off.

1.   The manager must strike an acceptable balance between holding too much or too little cash.

---

[1] John Maynard Keynes, *The General Theory of Employment Interest and Money* (New York: Harcourt Brace Jovanovich, Inc., 1936).

2. A large cash investment minimizes the chances of insolvency, but it penalizes company profitability.

3. A small cash investment frees excess (cash) balances for investment in longer-lived and more profitable assets, which increases the firm's profitability.

B. The firm's cash management system should strive to achieve two prime objectives.

1. Enough cash must be on hand to dispense effectively given the disbursal needs that arise in the course of doing business.

2. The firm's investment in idle cash balances must be reduced to a minimum.

C. In the attempt to meet the two objectives noted above, certain decisions dominate the cash-management process. These decision areas can be reduced to the following questions.

1. What can be done to speed up cash collections and slow down or better control cash outflows?

2. What should the composition of the marketable securities portfolio be?

IV. Collection and Disbursement Procedures

A. Cash acceleration and deceleration techniques revolve around the concept of **float.** Float can be broken down into four elements.

1. **Mail float** refers to funds that are tied up as a result of the time that elapses from the moment a customer mails a remittance check until the firm begins to process the check.

2. **Processing float** refers to funds that are tied up as a result of the firm's recording and processing remittance checks prior to their deposit in the bank.

3. **Transit float** refers to funds that are tied up as a result of the time needed for a deposited check to clear through the commercial banking system and become "usable" funds to the firm.

4. **Disbursing float** refers to funds that are technically usable to the firm until its *payment* check has cleared through the banking system and has been charged against its deposit account.

B. Float reduction can result in considerable benefits in terms of (1) usable funds that are released for company use and (2) in the returns produced on these freed-up balances. A study problem at the end of this chapter illustrates the calculation of such savings.

In October 28, 2004, the Check Clearing for the 21st Century Act took effect. This new law is commonly referred to as "Check 21." Prior to this regulation, ordinary paper checks were physically transported by land or air carrier from the depositing location to the financial institution that would eventually pay the check drawn against the firm's or individual's bank account.

Check 21 allow financial institutions the option of clearing a check image instead of the original check. Such digital substitutes can then be quickly processed within the banking clearing system in the same way that you use the internet on your personal computer. These digital substitutes are being referred to as substitute checks or image replacement documents.

The impetus for this new law was threefold: (1) bank regulators, like those at the Federal Reserve System, feel that Check 21 will accelerate check collection at the ultimate or payee bank; (2) it is forecast that out-of-pocket transportation costs to the banking system will be reduced, thus increasing individual bank profitability; and (3) the high degree of physical risk exposure associated with airline service can be minimized.

From the viewpoint of the firm's cash management system, "managing the float" will eventually be directly impacted by Check 21. What is called "disbursing float" above could be dramatically reduced towards a few hours instead of a day or two. Check 21 did not, however, require banks to alter their "hold" time on specific checks or substitute checks posted to the firm's account within the bank (these are ultimately cash inflows that become "good" funds).

So while the check may have cleared within the bank clearing mechanism, (i.e., from bank to bank), the firm may not have use of "good" funds until banks are forced by a yet-to-be-defined regulatory change to reduce their "hold" time on checks that have actually cleared. Thus, the effects of Check 21 on "transit float" (the third type of float mentioned above) will occur gradually as pressure is put on individual financial institutions to reduce hold times and make the funds available for disbursement by the receiving firm.

The upshot for the firm, and its cash management system, is that the greatest profitability opportunities are still associated with reducing mail float and processing float.

C. Several techniques are available to improve the management of the firm's cash inflows. These techniques may also provide for a reduction in float.

    1. The lock-box arrangement is a widely used commercial banking service for expediting cash gathering.

        a. The objective is to reduce *both* mail and processing float.

        b. The procedure behind a lock-box system is very simple. The firm rents a local post office box and authorizes a local bank in which a deposit account is maintained to pick up remittances from the box.

            (1) Customers are instructed to mail their payments to the numbered post office box.

            (2) A deposit form is prepared by the *bank* for each batch of processed checks.

            (3) The bank may notify the firm daily as to the amount of funds deposited on the firm's behalf.

            (4) The firm that receives checks from all over the country establishes several lock boxes.

        c. A lock-box arrangement provides for (1) increased working cash, (2) elimination of clerical functions, and (3) early knowledge of dishonored checks.

        d. The firm must carefully evaluate whether this or any cash management service is worth the added costs. Usually, the bank levies a charge for each check processed through the system. The marginal income generated from released funds must exceed the added costs of the system to make it economically beneficial. A study problem at the end of this chapter illustrates this kind of calculation.

D. Techniques used by firms that hope to improve the management of their cash outflows include: (1) zero balance accounts, (2) payable-through drafts, and (3) remote disbursing.

1. **Zero balance accounts** (ZBAs) permit centralized control (i.e., at the head office) over cash disbursements, but, at the same time, they allow the firm to maintain disbursing authority at the local or divisional level.

   a. The major objective of a ZBA system is to achieve better control over cash payments. A secondary benefit of this technique *might* be an increase in disbursement float.

   b. For the firm that has several operating units, the benefits from using a ZBA system include:

      (1) Centralized control over disbursements.

      (2) Reduction of time spent on superficial cash management activities.

      (3) Reduction of excess cash balances held in outlying accounts.

      (4) An increase in disbursement float.

2. **Payable-through drafts** (PTDs) have the physical appearance of ordinary checks but are drawn on and paid by the issuing firm instead of the bank. The bank serves as a collection point for the documents and passes the documents on to the firm for inspection and authorization for payment.

   a. The objective of a payable-through draft system is to provide for effective control of field authorized payments. An example would be a claim settlement authorized by an insurance agent.

   b. Stop payment orders can be initiated by the firm's head-quarters on any drafts considered inappropriate.

3. **Remote disbursing,** rather obviously, is intended to increase disbursing float.

    a. To implement such a procedure, the firm needs only to open and use a deposit account located in a city distant from its customers' banks.

    b. Since checks written on that account take longer to clear, the firm has use of its funds for a longer period of time.

    c. The major constraint on this procedure is the possible alienation of important customers who must wait longer for their remittance checks to become usable funds.

V. Evaluating the Costs of Cash Management Services

A. Whether a particular cash management system will provide an economic benefit to the firm can be evaluated by use of this relationship:

added costs = added benefits.

B. Clearly, if the benefits exceed the costs of using the system, then the system is economically feasible.

C. On a per-unit basis, this relationship can be expressed as follows:

$$P = (D)\,(S)\,(i)$$

where P = increase in per-check processing cost, if the new system is adopted,

    D = days saved in the collection process, (i.e., float reduction),

    S = average check size in dollars,

    i = the daily, before-tax opportunity cost (rate of return) of carrying cash.

D. The product of $(D)\,(S)\,(i)$ must exceed P for the system to be beneficial to the firm. A study problem at the end of this chapter provides an example of this logic.

VI.   Composition of the Marketable Securities Portfolio

A.   When selecting a proper marketable securities mix, five factors should be considered.

1.   **Financial risk** is the uncertainty of expected returns from a security due to unforeseeable changes in the financial capacity of the security issuer to make future payments to the security owner.

2.   **Interest rate risk** is the uncertainty in expected returns caused by possible changes in interest rates. This is particularly important for securities that have long, as opposed to short, terms of maturity. (See study problem 5 for an illustration of this point.)

3.   **Liquidity** is the ability to transform a security into cash. Consideration should be given to (1) the time needed to sell the security and (2) the likelihood that the security can be sold at or near its prevailing market price.

4.   The **taxability** of interest income and capital gains are seriously considered by some corporate treasurers.

   a.   The interest income from **municipal obligations** is tax-exempt.

   b.   The following equation may be used to determine an equivalent before-tax yield on a taxable security.

   (1)   Notation:

   r =   equivalent before-tax yield.

   r^* =   after-tax yield on tax-exempt security.

   T =   firm's marginal income tax rate.

   (2)   Computation

$$r = \frac{r^*}{(1-T)}$$

   (3)   Example: Suppose a firm has a choice between investing in a one-year, tax-free debt issue yielding 6% on a $1,000 outlay or a one-year, taxable issue that yields 7% on a $1,000 outlay. The firm pays

federal taxes at the rate of 34%. Which security is more beneficial to the firm?

$$r = \frac{0.06}{(1-0.34)} = 9.09\%$$

(4) Clearly, this firm should choose the tax-exempt security.

5. The **yield** criterion involves a weighing of the risks and benefits inherent in the four previously mentioned factors. The higher the risks associated with a particular security, the higher the expected yield (risk-return trade-off).

B. Marketable security alternatives

1. A **Treasury bill** is a direct obligation of the U.S. government sold on a regular basis by the U.S. Treasury.

   a. These bills may now be purchased in denominations as small as $1,000.

   b. Because Treasury bills are backed by the U.S. government, they are considered risk-free and consequently sell at lower yields than those obtainable on other marketable securities.

   c. The income from Treasury bills is subject only to federal income taxes and is always taxed as an ordinary gain.

2. **Federal agency securities** represent debt obligations of federal government agencies and were created to carry out lending programs of the U.S. government.

3. **Bankers' acceptances** are largely concentrated in the financing of foreign transactions; this acceptance is a draft (order to pay) drawn on a specific bank by an exporter in order to obtain payment for goods shipped to a customer who maintains an account with that bank.

4. A **negotiable certificate of deposit** (CD) is a marketable receipt for funds that have been deposited in a bank for a fixed time period at a fixed interest rate.

5. **Commercial paper** refers to short-term, unsecured promissory notes sold by large businesses in order to raise cash.

6. **Repurchase agreements** are legal contracts that involve the actual sale of securities by a borrower to the lender, with a commitment on the part of the borrower to repurchase the securities at the contract price plus a stated interest charge.

7. **Money market mutual funds** usually invest in a diversified portfolio of short-term, high-grade debt instruments like those described in this section.

   a. These funds sell their shares to a large number of small investors in order to raise cash.

   b. The funds offer the investing firm a high degree of liquidity and investment expertise.

VII. Accounts Receivable

A. Typically, accounts receivable represent just over 25% of a firm's assets.

B. The size of the investment in accounts receivable varies from industry to industry and is affected by several factors, including the percentage of credit sales to total sales, the level of sales, and the credit and collection policies—more specifically the terms of sale, the quality of customer, and collection efforts.

C. Although all these factors affect the size of the investment, only the credit and collection policies are decision variables under the control of the financial manager.

D. The terms of sale are generally stated in the form **a/b** net **c**, indicating that the customer can deduct **a** percentage if the account is paid within **b** days; otherwise, the account must be paid within **c** days.

E. If the customer decides to forgo the discount and not pay until the final payment date, the annualized opportunity cost of passing up this **a**% discount and withholding payment until the **c**th day is determined as follows:

$$\text{annualized opportunity cost of forgoing the discount} = \frac{a}{1-a} \times \frac{360}{c-b}$$

Example: Given the trade credit terms of 3/20 net 60, what is the annualized opportunity cost of passing up the 3% discount and withholding payment until the 60th day?

Solution: Substituting in the values from the example, we get

$$27.8\% = \frac{0.03}{1-0.03} \times \frac{360}{60-20}$$

F. A second decision variable in determining the size of the investment in accounts receivable, in addition to the trade credit terms, is the type of customer.

   1. The costs associated with extending credit to lower-quality customers include:

      a. Increased costs of credit investigation.

      b. Increased probability of customer default.

      c. Increased collection costs.

G. Analyzing the credit application is a major part of accounts receivable management.

   1. Several avenues are open to the firm in considering the credit rating of an applicant. Among these are financial statements, independent credit ratings and reports, bank checking, information from other companies, and past experiences.

   2. One commonly used method for credit evaluation is called credit scoring and involves the numerical evaluation of each applicant in which an applicant receives a score based on the answers to a simple set of questions. The score is then evaluated relative to a predetermined standard, determining whether or not credit scoring should be extended to the applicant. The major advantage of credit scoring is that it is inexpensive and easy to perform.

   3. Once the decision to extend credit has been made, a maximum credit line is established as a ceiling on the amount of credit to be extended.

H.   The third and final decision variable in determining the size of the investment in accounts receivable is the firm's collection policies.

   1.   Collection policy is a combination of letter sending, telephone calls, personal visits, and legal actions.

   2.   The greater the amount spent on collecting, the lower the volume of bad debts.

      a.   The relationship is not linear, however, and beyond a point is not helpful.

      b.   If sales are independent of collection efforts, then methods of collection should be evaluated with respect to the reduction in bad debts against the cost of lowering those bad debts.

I.   Credit should be extended to the point that marginal profitability on additional sales equals the required rate of return on the additional investment in receivables necessary to generate those sales.

J.   Credit policy changes involve direct trade-offs between costs and benefits. Determining whether the increased sales contribute toward more profits than the increased costs taken away from them is the job of marginal or incremental analysis. Marginal analysis is performed as follows.

   1.   Estimate the change in profits from the new policy. This is equal to the increased sales times the profit contribution less any additional bad debts incurred.

   2.   Estimate the cost of the additional investment in accounts receivable and inventory.

   3.   Estimate the change in the cost of the cash discount (if a change in the cash discount is enacted).

   4.   Compare the incremental revenues with the incremental costs.

VIII.   Inventory

   A.   Typically, inventory accounts for about 4.88% of a firm's assets.

B.   The purpose of carrying inventories is to uncouple the operations of the firm, that is, to make each function of the business independent of each other function.

C.   As such, the decision with respect to the size of the investment in inventory involves a basic trade-off between risk and return.

D.   The risk comes from the possibility of running out of inventory if too little inventory is held, while the return aspect of this trade-off results because increased inventory investment costs money.

E.   There are several general types of inventory.

    1.   Raw materials inventory consists of the basic materials that have been purchased from other firms to be used in the firm's productions operations. This type of inventory uncouples the production function from the purchasing function.

    2.   Work-in-process inventory consists of partially finished goods that require additional work before they become finished goods. This type of inventory uncouples the various production operations.

    3.   Finished goods inventory consists of goods on which the production has been completed but the goods are not yet sold. This type of inventory uncouples the production and sales function.

    4.   Stock of cash inventory serves to make the payment of bills independent of the collection of accounts due.

F.   In order to effectively manage the investment in inventory, two problems must be dealt with: the order quantity problem and the order point problem.

G.   The order quantity problem involves the determination of the optimal order size for an inventory item given its expected usage, carrying, and ordering costs.

H.   The economic order quantity (EOQ) model attempts to determine the order size that will minimize total inventory costs. The EOQ is given as:

$$Q^* = \sqrt{\frac{2SO}{C}}$$

where C   =   carrying costs per unit

$$O \quad = \quad \text{ordering costs per order}$$

$$S \quad = \quad \text{total demand in units over the planning period}$$

$$Q^* \quad = \quad \text{the optimal order quantity in units}$$

I.   The order point problem attempts to answer the following question: How low should inventory be depleted before it is reordered?

J.   In answering this question, two factors become important.

   1.   What is the usual procurement or delivery time, and how much stock is needed to accommodate this time period?

   2.   How much safety stock does the management desire?

K.   Modification for safety stocks is necessary, since the usage rate of inventory is seldom stable over a given timetable.

L.   This safety stock is used to safeguard the firm against changes in both order time and receipt of shipped goods.

M.   The greater the uncertainty associated with forecasted demand or order time, the larger the safety stock.

   1.   The costs associated with running out of inventory will also determine the safety stock levels.

   2.   A point is reached where it is too costly to carry a larger safety stock given the associated risk.

N.   Inflation can also have an impact on the level of inventory carried.

   1.   Goods may be purchased in large quantities in anticipation of price rises.

   2.   The cost of carrying goods may increase, causing a decline in Q^*, the optional order quantity.

O.   The just-in-time inventory control system is more than just an inventory control system; it is a production and management system.

   1.   Under this system, inventory is cut down to a minimum, and the time and physical distance between the various production operations are also minimized.

   2.   Actually, the just-in-time inventory control system is just a new approach to the EOQ model, which tries to produce the lowest average level of inventory possible.

3.   Average inventory is reduced by locating inventory supplies in convenient locations and setting up restocking strategies that cut time and thereby reduce the needed level of safety stock.

Study Problems

1.   Buckeye Equipment has $3,000,000 in excess cash that it might invest in marketable securities. In order to buy and sell the securities, though, the company must pay a transactions fee of $67,500.

    (a)   Would you recommend purchasing the securities if they yield 13% annually and are held for:

        1.   one month?
        2.   two months?
        3.   three months?
        4.   six months?
        5.   one year?

    (b)   What minimum required yield would the securities have to return for the firm to hold them for three months?

SOLUTION

    (a)   It is necessary to calculate the dollar value of the estimated return for each holding period and compare it with the transactions fee. This will allow you to determine if a gain can be made by investing in the securities. The calculations and recommendations are shown below.

			Recommendation
1. $3,000,000(.13)(1/12)	=	$32,500 < $67,500	No
2. $3,000,000(.13)(2/12)	=	$65,000 < $67,500	No
3. $3,000,000(.13)(3/12)	=	$97,500 > $67,500	Yes
4. $3,000,000(.13)(6/12)	=	$195,000 > $67,500	Yes
5. $3,000,000(.13)(12/12)	=	$390,000 > $67,500	Yes

    (b)   Now we find the break-even yield for a three-month holding period. Let (%) be the required yield. With $3,000,000 to invest for three months, we have:

$$\$3,000,000 \ (\%) \ (3/12) = \$67,500$$
$$\$3,000,000 \ (\%) = \$270,000$$
$$(\%) = \$270,000/\$3,000,000 = \underline{9\%}$$

2.   Portland Energy Products is evaluating whether or not to use an additional lock box. If the lock box is used, check processing costs will rise by $.20 a check. The average check size that will be mailed to the lock-box location is $1,000. Funds that are freed by using the lock box will be invested in marketable securities to yield an *annual* before-tax return of 7%. The firm uses a 365-day year in its analysis procedures. What reduction in check-collection time is required to justify use of the lock box?

SOLUTION

Solve the following relationship for D:

$$P = (D)\ (S)\ (i)$$

$$\$.20 = (D)(\$1,000)\left(\frac{0.07}{365}\right)$$

$$\$.20 = (D)\ (\$.192)$$

$$\frac{\$.20}{\$.192} = D = \underline{1.0417\ days}$$

Thus, the lock box is justified if it can speed up collections by *more* than 1.0417 days.

3.   Annual sales for Austin Drilling Supply will total $250,000,000 next year. What would be the annual value of one day's float reduction to this firm if it could invest the freed-up balances at 8% per year?

SOLUTION

Compute Austin's sales per day:

$$\frac{\text{annual revenues}}{\text{days in years}} = \frac{250,000,000}{365} = \$684,932$$

Compute the annual value of the one-day float reduction:

$$(\$684,932)\ (0.08) = \underline{\$54,795}$$

4.   The corporate treasurer of Buckeye Bottling is considering purchasing a municipal obligation with a 7% coupon and a $1,000 par value. Mr. Inside Info has telephoned the treasurer about another $1,000 par value offering that provides a 12% yield. This latter offering is, however, fully taxable. Buckeye is taxed at a 48% rate.

  (a)   Should the treasurer take Mr. Info's advice and purchase the 12% security?

  (b)   What is the equivalent before-tax yield on the municipal, assuming Buckeye is in a 48% tax bracket?

SOLUTION

  (a)   The after-tax yield to Buckeye on the 12% offering is (0.12) (1-0.48) = 6.24%. Since the yield on the municipal is already stated on an after-tax basis, the treasurer should ignore Mr. Info's advice and purchase the municipal offering.

  (b)   The equivalent before-tax yield is:

$$ r = \frac{0.07}{(1\text{-}0.48)} = \underline{13.46\%} $$

        Thus, the taxable issue would have to yield in excess of 13.46% to be more attractive than the municipal to Buckeye.

5.   Tech Electronics, manufacturers of fine calculators, has recently purchased 10-year bonds at their par value of $1,000 per security. Texas Parts, a close competitor, has just purchased five-year bonds at their $1,000 par value. Both securities have a coupon rate set at 8%, are compounded annually, and have a maturity value of $1,000. Suppose the prevailing interest rate one year from now rises to 10%. What would the decline in market price be for each bond in one year?

SOLUTION

One year from now, the five-year issue has four years remaining to maturity. The market price in one year can be found by computing P according to the following:

$$P = \sum_{t=1}^{4} \frac{\$80}{(1 + 0.10)^t} + \frac{\$1,000}{(1+0.10)^4} = \$936.60$$

where $\$80 = (0.08)(\$1,000)$. Similarly, for the l0-year issue, which now has nine years to maturity,

$$P = \sum_{t=1}^{9} \frac{\$80}{(1 + 0.10)^t} + \frac{\$1,000}{(1+0.10)^9} = \$884.82.$$

Thus the 10-year security declines in price $115.18 ($1,000 - $884.82), while the five-year security declines in price by only $63.40 ($1,000 – $936.60). This illustrates the concept of *interest rate risk*, discussed in the text in Chapter 15.

6. Gavin International expects to generate sales of $74,000,000 in the coming year. All sales are done on a credit basis, net 30 days. Gavin has estimated that it takes an average of four days for payments to reach their central office and an additional day to process the payments. What is the opportunity cost of the funds tied up in the mail and processing? Gavin uses a 360-day year in all calculations and can invest free funds at 7%.

SOLUTION

Daily collections = 74,000,000/360 = $ 205,555.56

Opportunity Cost = (205,555.56) (5) (.07) = $71,944

7. The corporate treasurer of Chester Motors is considering the purchase of either an offering carrying a 7.6% coupon or a municipal obligation with a 5% coupon. Both bonds have a $1,000 par value. The company is currently in the 34% marginal tax bracket. Which security should the treasurer recommend?

SOLUTION

The after-tax yield to Chester Motors on the 7.6% offering is (1 – .34) (.076) = 5%. The municipal's after-tax rate is the stated 5%. There is no difference in yield. If the risk is considered equal for each security, then the treasurer would be indifferent between the two.

8.   The Swank Furniture Company is trying to determine the optimal order quantity for sofas. Annual sales for sofas are 800, and the retail price is $300 per sofa. The cost of carrying sofas is $50 per sofa per year. It costs $35 to prepare and receive an order. The inventory planning period is one year.

(a)   Determine the EOQ (assuming a one-year planning period).

(b)   If the annual sales are 1200, what is the EOQ? If the annual sales are 300, what is the EOQ?

SOLUTION

(a) $EOQ = \sqrt{\dfrac{2(800)(35)}{50}} = \sqrt{1120} = 33.47 = 33$ sofas

(b) $EOQ = \sqrt{\dfrac{2(1200)(35)}{50}} = \sqrt{1680} = 40.99 = 41$ sofas

$\sqrt{\dfrac{2(300)(35)}{50}} = \sqrt{420} = 20.49 = 20$ sofas

9.   What is the effective annualized cost of forgoing a trade discount with terms 4/40, net 60?

SOLUTION

$$\text{The annualized opportunity cost of forgoing the trade discount} = \frac{a}{1-a} \times \frac{360}{c-b}$$

where the terms of sale are stated in the form **a/b** net **c**, indicating that they can deduct **a**% if the account is paid within **b** days; otherwise, the account must be paid within **c** days.

Thus,
$$\text{annualized opportunity cost of forgoing the trade discount} = \frac{a}{1-a} \times \frac{360}{c-b}$$

$$= \frac{.04}{1-.04} \times \frac{360}{6040}$$

$$= 0.75$$

$$= 75\%$$

<u>Self Tests</u>

TRUE-FALSE

_____ 1. Accounts receivable are included on the balance sheet as current liabilities.

_____ 2. Holding cash to pay for next week's labor bill (payroll) is an example of the precautionary motive for holding cash.

_____ 3. Ready borrowing power enables the firm to reduce the cash balances actually held for precautionary purposes.

_____ 4. A firm is insolvent when it is able to meet its short-term obligations on time.

_____ 5. Cash flow forecasting is the initial step in any effective cash management program.

_____ 6. The major objective of using payable-through drafts is to extend disbursing float.

_____ 7. The major reason for using lock boxes is to enjoy a reduction in transit float.

_____ 8. Zero balance accounts are used to accelerate cash receipts.

_____ 9. Although they have a lower yield, agency securities are more readily marketable by the purchasing corporation than Treasury bills are.

_____ 10. Bankers' acceptances generally mature from 9 to 12 months after "sight."

_____ 11. Commercial paper is backed by specific assets of the firm.

_____ 12. The most common denomination for the negotiable CD is $10,000.

_____ 13. The longer the term of maturity, the less sensitive the price of a security to changes in interest rates.

_____ 14. Long-term bonds may serve as a useful (comfortable) hedge against interest rate risk.

_____ 15. Because of their higher financial risk, agency securities always yield more than Treasury securities of a comparable maturity.

_____ 16. The higher the marginal tax bracket, the lower the after-tax rate of return on a taxable security.

_____ 17. Bankers' acceptances provide for a steady flow of interest payments to the investor in the form of coupon payments.

_____ 18. With respect to interest risk, Treasury securities are risk-free.

_____ 19. The lock-box system is the most widely used commercial banking service for expediting cash gathering.

_____ 20. A concentration bank is one where the firm generally maintains several minor disbursing accounts.

_____ 21. There is an inverse relationship between a financial instrument's chance of default and financial risk.

_____ 22. The contract price of the securities that make up the repurchase agreement is fixed for the duration of the transaction.

_____ 23. According to Keynes, the demand for cash can be divided into three categories: transactions, precautionary, and speculative.

_____ 24. To calculate the annual savings due to float reduction, you would multiply the sales per day by the days of float reduction.

_____ 25. Payable-through drafts provide control over field payments.

_____ 26. Increases in cash holdings from external sources of funds tend to be more regular than internal generation of cash.

_____ 27. The motives for holding cash apply equally to all firms. Variations in cash holdings from firm to firm result from differing management risk preferences.

_____ 28. The prime objectives of cash management are to reduce idle cash balances and to have sufficient cash on hand to meet disbursal needs.

_____ 29. Under the lock-box arrangement, a deposit form is prepared by the *depositor* for each batch of processed checks.

_____ 30. The use of payable-through drafts will usually increase disbursing float to the issuing firm.

_____ 31. The expression "5/10, net 30" means that the customers receive a 10% discount if they pay within 5 days; otherwise, they must pay within 30 days.

_____ 32. There is no one level of inventory that is efficient for all firms.

_____ 33. In determining the level of safety stock, it is important to evaluate the trade-off between the cost of carrying the additional inventory with the risk of running out of inventory.

_____ 34. The EOQ provides for an optimal safety stock determination.

MULTIPLE CHOICE

1. Which of the following is not an advantage of the lock-box system?

    a. The cost is minimal.
    b. Speeds up the flow of cash to the firm.
    c. Remittances are collected sooner.
    d. All of the above are advantages.

2. Generally, the least important component of a firm's preference for liquidity is

    a. the transaction motive.
    b. the precautionary motive.
    c. the speculative motive.
    d. All motives are of equal importance.

3. Which of the following is *not* an objective of the lockbox system?

    a. Reduce mail float.
    b. Reduce processing float.
    c. Reduce transit float.
    d. Reduce disbursing float.

4. The fact that funds are not available in the company's bank account until its payment check has cleared through the banking system refers to

    a. mail float.
    b. processing float.
    c. transit float.
    d. disbursing float.

5. Interest rate risk is of concern to a firm's financial officer, because

    a. it is more difficult to issue securities when interest rates are low.
    b. changes in interest rates affect the expected return of financial instruments.
    c. federal government taxation increases as interest rates rise, reducing the cash available to the firm.
    d. inflationary periods may reduce the real earnings of the firm.

6. Which of the following is *not* a motive for holding cash balances?

    a. transactions motive
    b. speculative motive
    c. convenience motive
    d. precautionary motive

7. A concentration bank is

    a. a bank that has the most deposit accounts.
    b. a bank that concentrates its service in one geographic area.
    c. a bank that concentrates on one type of service.
    d. a bank in which the firm maintains a major disbursing account.
    e. none of the above.

8. Which of the following is not part of the firm's credit and collection policy decisions?

    a. the credit period
    b. the cash discount given
    c. the dividend decision
    d. the level of collection expenditures
    e. none of the above

9. Which of the following is not a characteristic of a firm's safety stock of inventory?

    a. The greater the risk of running out of stock, the larger the safety stock.
    b. The larger the opportunity cost of the funds invested in inventory, the smaller the safety stock.
    c. The greater the uncertainty associated with future forecasts of use, the larger the safety stock.
    d. The higher the profit margin per unit, the lower the safety stock necessary.
    e. None of the above are true.

10. In the basic model, the optimal inventory level is the point at which

    a. total depreciation is minimized.
    b. total cost is minimized.
    c. total revenue is maximized.
    d. carrying costs are minimized.
    e. None of the above are true.

CHAPTER 17

International Business Finance

<u>Orientation</u>: This chapter introduces some of the financial techniques and strategies necessary for the efficient operation of an international business. Problems inherent to these firms include multiple currencies, differing legal and political environments, differing economic and capital markets, and internal control problems. The difficulties arising from multiple currencies are stressed here, including the dimensions of foreign exchange risk and strategies for reducing this risk. We also cover working-capital management and direct foreign investment for international firms.

I. The Globalization of Product and Financial Markets

   A. World trade has grown faster over the last few decades than has aggregate world GNP.

   B. In less-developed countries, long-run overseas investments by U.S. companies have yielded high returns.

   C. Many American **multinational corporations** (MNC) have significant assets, sales, and profits attributable to foreign investments.

   D. Many foreign MNCs have significant operations in the United States.

   E. Many firms, investment companies, and individuals invest in the capital markets of foreign companies in the hopes of realizing

      1. higher returns than those available in domestic capital markets, and

      2. reduced portfolio risk through international diversification.

   F. Companies are increasingly turning to the Eurodollar market to raise funds.

II.   Exchange Rates

    A.   Recent history of exchange rates

        1.   Exchange rates between the major currencies were fixed from 1949 until 1970.

        2.   Countries were required to set a **parity rate** with the U.S. dollar, around which the daily exchange rate could narrowly fluctuate.

        3.   In order to effect a major adjustment, a currency had to undergo either a **devaluation** (reducing the cost relative to the dollar) or an **up-valuation/revaluation** (increasing the cost relative to the U.S. dollar).

        4.   Since 1973, a **floating rate** international currency system has operated, wherein the currencies are allowed to fluctuate freely.

        5.   Two major types of transactions now occur in the foreign exchange markets: **spot** and **forward transactions.**

    B.   Spot exchange rates

        1.   The rate at which one currency can be immediately exchanged for another currency

        2.   **Direct quote** expresses the exchange rate in the units of home currency required to buy one unit of foreign currency. For example, 1.4845 U.S. dollars per pound.

        3.   **Indirect quotes** indicate the number of foreign currency units needed to purchase one unit of home currency. For example, .6691 pounds per U.S. dollar.

        EXAMPLE

        Using the rates listed above, how many dollars would a U.S. manufacturer pay for a part costing 250 pounds?

        250 (pounds) x 1.4845 ($/pound) = $371.13

4. The direct and indirect quotes should have a reciprocal relationship. In formula

$$\text{Direct Quote} = \frac{1}{\text{Indirect Quote}}$$

or

$$\text{Indirect Quote} = \frac{1}{\text{Direct Quote}}$$

5. When these quotes are not equal, **arbitrage** will occur, where a trader (or arbitrageur) makes a riskless profit by exchanging currency in two markets.

6. The **asked rate** is the rate which the bank or foreign exchange trader "asks" the buyer to pay for the foreign currency.

7. The **bid rate** is the rate at which the bank or foreign exchange trader buys the foreign currency from the customer.

8. The **spread** is the difference in the bid and the asked rates.

9. The narrower the spread, the greater the efficiency in the spot exchange market.

10. A **cross rate** is the result of an indirect computation of one currency's exchange rate from the exchange rate of two other currencies. For example, the calculation of marks per pound from U.S. dollars per pound and marks per U.S. dollars.

C. Forward exchange rates

1. A **forward exchange rate** specifies *today* the rate at which currencies will be exchanged in the future, usually 30, 90, or 180 days from today.

2. Rates are quoted in both the direct and indirect form.

3. Forward rates are often quoted at a **premium** or a **discount** to the existing spot rate. This is also referred to as the forward-spot differential.

4.   These differentials may be stated either in absolute terms or as an annualized percent premium or discount.

5.   The use of forward contracts allows for risk reduction, in that future cash outlays are known with certainty.

III.   Interest Rate Parity

A.   Theorem states that the forward premium or discount should be equal and opposite in sign to the difference in the national interest rates for securities of the same maturity (except for the effects of small transaction costs). Notationally, this is expressed as

$$P \text{ (or D)} \quad = \quad -\left(\frac{I^f - I^d}{1 + I^f}\right) = \left(\frac{I^d - I^f}{1 + I^f}\right)$$

where

P (or D) = the percent-per-annum premium or discount on the forward rate

I^f =   the annual interest rate on a foreign instrument having the same maturity as the forward contract

I^d =   the annualized interest rate on a domestic instrument having the same maturity as the forward contract

EXAMPLE

The premium (P) on 30-day forward mark contracts is 4.368%. If the 30-day T-bill is yielding 10%, what must the 30-day German instrument yield?

$$P \quad = \quad \left(\frac{I^f - I^d}{1 + I^f}\right)$$

$$0.04368 \quad = \quad \frac{I^f - .10}{1 + I^f}$$

$$I^f \quad = \quad .1502 \text{ or } 15.02\%$$

B.   If the forward differentials are not those predicted by the interest parity theorem, then **covered interest arbitrage** can occur and be profitable at no risk.

IV. Purchasing Power Parity

A. According to purchasing power parity, exchange rates will adjust over time so that the currencies of different countries will have the same purchasing power. The exchange rates will adjust to cover the inflation rate differential between the two countries.

B. Purchasing power parity can be demonstrated by the equation

$$S_{t+1} = S_t (1 + P_d) / (1 + P_f)^n$$

$$= S_t (1 + P_d - P_f)^n$$

where

S_t = units of domestic currency per unit of the foreign currency at time t,

P_f = the foreign inflation rate,

P_d = the domestic inflation rate, and

n = the number of time periods.

EXAMPLE

The inflation rate is 6% in Great Britain and 10% in the United States. The current spot rate of the pound is $2.00. According to purchasing power parity, what will be the expected value of the British pound at the end of the year?

$$S = \$2.00 (1 + .10 - .06)^1$$

$$= \$2.00 (1.04)^1$$

$$= \$2.08$$

C. The law of one price

The law of one price underlies purchasing power parity. This law suggests that where there are no transportation costs or barriers to trade, the same good sold in different countries should sell for the same price if all the different prices are expressed in terms of the same currency.

D.   International Fisher effect

1.   According to the Fisher effect, interest rates reflect not only the real rate of return but also the expected inflation rate.

2.   The Fisher effect can be expressed as

$$= \quad P + I_r + (P)(I_r)$$

$$r_{nom} \quad = \quad r_{inf} + r_{real} + (r_{inf})(r_{real})$$

where

$$r_{nom} \quad = \quad \text{the nominal interest rate}$$

$$r_{real} \quad = \quad \text{the real rate of return}$$

$$r_{inf} \quad = \quad \text{the expected inflation rate}$$

3.   The international Fisher effect suggests that the exchange rate adjusts to cover the interest rate differential between two countries.

4.   This theory suggests that in efficient markets, with rational expectations, the forward rate is an unbiased forecast of the future spot rate.

V.   Exchange Rate Risk

A.   Risk arises from not knowing today the value of the future spot rate.

B.   Types of exchange risk

1.   **Risk in international trade contracts:** When an agreement exists to purchase some good at a future date in foreign currency, uncertainty exists as to the future cash outlay.

2.   **Risk in foreign portfolios:** Because of exchange rate fluctuations in foreign securities, the returns are more variable, and thus, more risky than investment in domestic securities.

3.   **Risk in direct foreign investment (DFI):** The balance sheet and income statement are dominated in foreign currency. Thus for the parent company, risk arises from the fluctuations in both the asset's value and the profit streams.

C.   Exposure to exchange rate risk

1.   Transaction exposure refers to the net total foreign currency transactions whose monetary value was fixed at a time different from when the transactions are actually completed. Examples of transactions exposed to this kind of risk are receivables, payables, and fixed price sales or purchase contracts. Fluctuations in exchange rates can affect the value of these assets and liabilities.

2.   Translation exposure is actually a paper gain or loss. Translation exposure refers to gains or losses caused by the translation of foreign currency assets and liabilities into the currency of the parent company for accounting purposes.

3.   Economic exposure refers to the extent to which the economic value of a company can decline due to exchange rate changes. It is the overall impact of exchange rate changes on the value of the firm. A decline in value can be attributed to an exchange-rate-induced decline in the level of expected cash flows and/or by an increase in the riskiness of these cash flows.

D.   Hedging strategies

1.   The standard procedure to hedge is to match the amount and the duration of the asset (liability) position.

2.   The **money market hedge** offsets the exposed position in a foreign currency by borrowing or lending in the foreign and domestic money markets. This may be costly for small or infrequent users.

3.   The **forward market hedge** matches the asset (liability) position with an offsetting forward contract of equal value and maturity. Generally, this is less costly than the money market hedge.

4.   Foreign currency futures contracts and foreign currency options are two relatively new instruments used for hedging. Futures contracts are similar to forward contracts in that they provide a fixed price for the required delivery. Options, on the other hand, *permit* a fixed price anytime before their expiration date. Options and futures both differ from forward contracts in that they are traded in standardized amounts with standardized maturity dates and are traded through organized exchanges and individual dealers. The difference between the futures contract and the

currency option is that the option requires delivery only if it is exercised. The option can be exercised anytime before its maturity date; this can provide additional flexibility for a company.

VI. Multinational Working-Capital Management

A. The MNC must be careful to make decisions concerning working-capital management that are optimal for the corporation as a whole and not just the best for the individual entities.

B. **Leading** and **lagging** are important risk reduction techniques for a MNC's working-capital management.

1. When holding an *asset* in a

a. strong (appreciating) currency, we should lag (delay) conversion to the domestic currency.

b. weak (depreciating) currency, we should lead (expedite) conversion to the domestic currency.

2. When holding a *liability* in a

a. strong currency, we should lead (expedite) payment of the liability.

b. weak currency, we should lag (delay) payment of the liability.

C. Cash management

1. An MNC may wish to position funds in a specific subsidiary in another country such that the foreign exchange exposure and the tax liability of the MNC are minimized as a whole. This strategy may not, however, be the optimal strategy for the subsidiary.

2. The transfer of funds is effected by royalties, fees, and transfer-pricing. The **transfer price** is the price charged for goods or services transferred from a subsidiary or parent company to another subsidiary.

VII. International Financing Decisions

A. A multinational corporation (MNC) may have a lower cost of capital than a domestic firm due to its ability to tap a larger number of financial markets.

1. A multinational company has access to financing sources in the countries in which it operates.

2. Host countries often provide access to low-cost, subsidized financing to attract foreign investment.

3. An MNC may enjoy preferential credit treatment due to its size and investor preference for its home currency.

4. An MNC may be able to access third country capital markets.

5. An MNC has access to external currency markets variously known as Eurodollar, Eurocurrency, or Asian dollar markets. These markets are unregulated and, because of their lower spread, can offer attractive rates for financing and investment.

B. To increase their visibility in foreign capital markets, MNCs are increasingly listing their stocks in the foreign capital markets.

C. An MNC's capital structure should reflect its wider access to financial markets, the ability to diversify economic and political risks, and several of its other advantages over domestic firms.

VIII. Direct Foreign Investment

A. Risk in international capital budgeting

1. Political risk arises from operating a business in a different and possibly less stable business climate than the United States.

2. Exchange risk incorporates changes in the future earnings stream because of currency fluctuations, possibly in both foreign and domestic currencies.

3. Business risk is affected by the response of business and the MNC to economic conditions within the foreign country.

4. Financial risk arises from the financial structure of the firm and its effect on the profit stream.

B. Cash flows must be estimated considering the potential effects of exchange rate changes, governmental policy, and other items that determine product demand and sales.

C. A foreign investment can be evaluated from either a parent or a local firm perspective. If a firm uses a local perspective, the initial investment and all of its cash flows should be discounted at a rate that reflects the local inflation rate and the riskiness of the project. When using the parent company perspective, the discount rate should reflect the expected inflation rate in the parent currency, and foreign currency cash flows should be converted to the parent currency cash flows using projected exchange rates.

D. The net present value (NPV) must be calculated using the preceding factors.

   1. If NPV is greater than zero, accept direct foreign investments.

   2. If NPV is less than zero, the MNC may decide to

      a. Reject direct foreign investment.

      b. Establish a sales office in the foreign country.

      c. License a local company to manufacture the product, where the MNC receives royalty payments.

Study Problems

1. An American manufacturer owes 5,000 marks to a German supplier. How much does he owe in U.S. dollars, if the exchange rate is 0.661 U.S. dollars per mark?

SOLUTION

   Exchange rate = 0.6601 U.S. dollar per mark

   5,000 (marks) x 0.6601 (U.S. dollar/mark) = $3,300.50 U.S. dollars

2. A fashion designer in France owes $65,000, due in 30 days, to a counterpart in the United States. How much is the foreign liability today if the exchange rate for 30-day forward contracts is 5.2070 francs per U.S. dollar?

SOLUTION

   30-day forward exchange rate – 5.2070 francs per U.S. dollar

   65,000 ($) x 5.2070 (francs per U.S. dollar) = 338,455 francs

3. You own $20,000. The dollar rate in London is 0.5201. The pound rate is given in the textbook. Are arbitrage profits possible? Set up an arbitrage scheme with your capital. What is the gain (loss) in dollars?

SOLUTION

The London rate is 0.5201 pounds/U.S. dollar. The indirect New York rate is 0.5349 pounds/U.S. dollar.

Assuming no transaction costs, the rates between London and New York are out of line. Arbitrage profits are possible.

Pounds are cheaper in New York. Buy pounds in New York with the $20,000.

   20,000 ($) x .5349 (pounds/dollars) = 10,698 pounds.

Sell pounds in London.

   10,698 (pounds) ÷ .5201 (pounds/U.S. dollars) = $20,569.12.

Your net gain is $20,569.12 − $20,000 = $569.12

4.   Interest rates on the 30-day instruments in the United States and Germany are 12% and 10% (annualized), respectively. What is the correct price of the 30-day forward mark? Use spot rates from textbook.

SOLUTION

The spot rate is .6601 U.S. dollar per mark. The annual premium via equation discussed on page 276 is

$$= \frac{.12 - .10}{1 + .10} = \frac{.02}{1.10} = .0182$$

$$P = 1.82\%$$

Using this premium in equation (16-2), compute the "correct" forward price.

$$\frac{F - .6601}{.6601} \times \frac{12}{1} = .0182 \quad \underline{F = .6611}$$

<u>Self Tests</u>

TRUE-FALSE

_____   1.   One of the most difficult aspects of operating a business in a foreign country is the problem of multiple currencies.

_____   2.   International business affairs affect very few firms and, therefore, are of little concern to most businesses.

_____   3.   Exchange rates are fixed according to the U.S. dollar and must be maintained within a narrow margin unless a major adjustment is enacted.

_____   4.   The forward contract states the exchange rate to be used in the spot market on a specific date in the near future.

_____   5.   A narrow spread between the bid and asked rates indicates an efficient spot market.

_____   6.   The interest parity theorem states that (except for effect of transaction costs) the forward premium or discount should be equal and opposite in sign to the difference in the respective country's interest rates for securities of the same maturities.

_____   7.   Extensive profit opportunities exist for arbitrageurs in the foreign exchange markets.

_____   8.   Exchange rate risk constitutes only a small portion of the risk associated with international business.

_____   9.   An investor with foreign currency liabilities may want to hedge against exchange rate changes in the money markets.

_____ 10.   Leading and lagging are strategies for optimal working capital management.

_____ 11.   Covered interest arbitrage can be taken advantage of when the premiums in the forward rate are not equal to the interest rate differentials.

_____ 12.   Purchasing power parity suggests that exchange rates in countries with high inflation rates tend to decline.

_____ 13. Translation exposure results in exchange-rate-related losses or gains that have little or no impact on taxable income.

_____ 14. Futures contracts are customized with regard to the amount and maturity date of the contract.

_____ 15. Receivables and payables are subject to transaction exposure.

_____ 16. The objective of a hedging strategy is to have a positive net asset position in the foreign currency.

MULTIPLE CHOICE

1. A direct 30-day forward quote of 1.4957 U.S. dollars per British pound is equivalent to what 30-day indirect quote?

   a. .6686 U.S. dollars per British pound
   b. .6671 British pounds per U.S. dollar
   c. 1.4957 U.S. dollars per British pound
   d. .6686 British pounds per U.S. dollar
   e. .6671 British pounds per U.S. dollar

2. An example of a cross rate, when the exchange rates are given in U.S. dollars, would be

   a. marks per U.S. dollar.
   b. pounds per yen.
   c. yen per mark.
   d. U.S. dollars per yen.
   e. both b and c.

3. Forward rate contracts are used in international transactions to

   a. reduce the risk for the buyer.
   b. reduce the risk for the seller.
   c. both a and b
   d. neither a nor b

4.   If an investor noticed a discrepancy in the exchange rates of two countries and acted upon it, he would be engaging in

   a.   money market hedging.
   b.   forward hedging.
   c.   arbitrage.
   d.   sabotage.
   e.   leading strategies.

5.   If your firm held liabilities in a strong currency, it would be wise to

   a.   lead.
   b.   lag.
   c.   engage in money market hedging.
   d.   engage in forward hedging.
   e.   do all of the above.

6.   Direct foreign investment involves

   a.   political risk.
   b.   business risk.
   c.   financial risk.
   d.   exchange rate risk.
   e.   all of the above.

7.   If the net present value of a direct foreign investment project for an MNC is less than zero, they should

   a.   reject it.
   b.   open a sales office.
   c.   license a foreign company.
   d.   accept it.
   e.   a, b, and c are all possibilities.

8.   If the U.S. experiences a 7% inflation rate while France is experiencing a 4% inflation rate, then according to purchasing power parity,

   a.   the value of the U.S. dollar should increase by approximately 3% against the French franc.
   b.   the U.S. dollar should decline against the French franc by 3%.
   c.   the French franc would decline by 3% against the U.S. dollar.
   d.   there would be no change in either currency.

9. A paper loss/gain best describes which type of risk?

    a. economic.
    b. transaction.
    c. interest rate.
    d. translation.

10. Which of the following does not provide a hedge against some risk?

    a. forward contract
    b. money market hedge
    c. currency options
    d. futures contracts
    e. All are forms of hedging.

ANSWERS TO SELF TESTS

Chapter 1

True-False

1.	F	2.	T	3.	F	4.	T	5.	T
6.	F	7.	F	8.	F	9.	T	10.	F
11.	T								

Multiple Choice

1.	d	2.	e	3.	e	4.	e	5.	d
6.	d	7.	c	8.	d				

Chapter 2

True-False

1.	F	2.	T	3.	F	4.	F	5.	F
6.	F	7.	T	8.	T	9.	F	10.	T
11.	T	12.	F	13.	T	14.	F	15.	F
16.	T	17.	T	18.	F	19.	F	20.	T
21.	F	22.	T	23.	F	24.	F	25.	T
26.	F	27.	T	28.	T	29.	F		

Multiple Choice

1.	c	2.	d	3.	e	4.	b	5.	b
6.	a	7.	c	8.	d	9.	c	10.	c
11.	d	12.	b	13.	b	14.	c	15.	c
16.	d	17.	d	18.	b	19.	d	20.	c
21.	c	22.	c	23.	c	24.	b	25.	c

Chapter 3

True-False

1.	F	2.	T	3.	F	4.	T	5.	T
6.	F	7.	F	8.	F	9.	F	10.	T
11.	F	12.	T						

Multiple Choice

1.	d	2.	a	3.	b	4.	d	5.	d
6.	d	7.	b	8.	a	9.	c		

Chapter 4

True-False

1.	T	2.	F	3.	F	4.	T	5.	F
6.	T	7.	T	8.	F	9.	T	10.	T
11.	F	12.	F	13.	F	14.	F	15.	F

Multiple Choice

1.	b	2.	e	3.	c	4.	a	5.	e
6.	b	7.	b	8.	c	9.	b	10.	a

Chapter 5

True-False

1.	T	2.	T	3.	F	4.	T	5.	T
6.	T	7.	T	8.	F	9.	T	10.	F

Multiple Choice

1.	a	2.	c	3.	d	4.	c	5.	a

Chapter 6

True-False

1.	T	2.	T	3.	T	4.	F	5.	F
6.	F	7.	T	8.	T	9.	F	10.	F
11.	F	12.	F						

Multiple Choice

1.	b	2.	d	3.	c	4.	d	5.	b
6.	d	7.	b	8.	b	9.	a		

Chapter 7

True-False

1.	T	2.	F	3.	T	4.	T	5.	F
6.	T	7.	F	8.	T	9.	T	10.	F
11.	F	12.	F	13.	F	14.	F	15.	F
16.	T	17.	F	18.	T				

Multiple Choice

1.	a	2.	e	3.	a	4.	b	5.	b
6.	c	7.	c	8.	a	9.	b	10.	d
11.	b	12.	a	13.	b	14.	b	15.	d
16.	c	17.	e						

Chapter 8

True-False

1.	T	2.	T	3.	F	4.	F	5.	F
6.	F	7.	F	8.	F	9.	F	10.	F
11.	T	12.	F	13.	F	14.	F	15.	T

Multiple Choice

1. a	2. b	3. d	4. c	5. a
6. c	7. a	8. b	9. c	10. d
11. d	12. b			

Chapter 9

True-False

1. T	2. F	3. T	4. F	5. T
6. F	7. T	8. T	9. T	10. F

Multiple Choice

1. d	2. d	3. d	4. b	5. b
6. b	7. a	8. b	9. a	10. a

Chapter 10

True-False

1. T	2. T	3. T	4. T	5. F
6. T	7. T	8. F	9. T	10. T

Multiple Choice

1. c	2. d	3. e	4. d

Chapter 11

True-False

1. T	2. T	3. F	4. T	5. F
6. T	7. T	8. T		

Multiple Choice

1. c	2. d	3. e	4. d

Chapter 12

True-False

1.	F	2.	F	3.	T	4.	T	5.	T
6.	F	7.	T	8.	F	9.	F	10.	F
11.	F	12.	T	13.	T	14.	T	15.	T
16.	T	17.	T	18.	T	19.	F	20.	F
21.	T	22.	T	23.	T	24.	F	25.	T
26.	F	27.	F	28.	T	29.	F	30.	F
31.	F	32.	F	33.	T	34.	F	35.	F
36.	T	37.	T	38.	F	39.	F	40.	F
41.	T	42.	F						

Multiple Choice

1.	c	2.	c	3.	b	4.	b	5.	b
6.	b	7.	c	8.	b	9.	c	10.	d
11.	b	12.	d	13.	b	14.	b	15.	c
16.	e	17.	b	18.	d	19.	b	20.	b
21.	d	22.	b	23.	d	24.	e	25.	b
26.	e								

Chapter 13

True-False

1.	T	2.	F	3.	F	4.	F	5.	T
6.	F	7.	T	8.	T	9.	F	10.	F
11.	F	12.	F						

Multiple Choice

1.	b	2.	d	3.	d	4.	c	5.	d
6.	d	7.	d	8.	d	9.	e	10.	e
11.	b	12.	b	13.	d				

Chapter 14

True-False

1.	T	2.	T	3.	F	4.	T	5.	F
6.	T	7.	F	8.	F	9.	T	10.	F

Multiple Choice

1.	c	2.	e	3.	e	4.	c	5.	e

Chapter 15

True-False

1.	F	2.	F	3.	T	4.	F	5.	T
6.	T	7.	F	8.	T	9.	F	10.	T
11.	F	12.	F	13.	T	14.	F	15.	F
16.	T	17.	F	18.	F	19.	T		

Multiple Choice

1.	d	2.	e	3.	c	4.	a	5.	c
6.	e	7.	c	8.	b	9.	a	10.	c

Chapter 16

True-False

1. F	2. F	3. T	4. T	5. T
6. F	7. F	8. F	9. F	10. F
11. F	12. F	13. F	14. F	15. T
16. T	17. F	18. F	19. T	20. F
21. F	22. T	23. T	24. F	25. T
26. F	27. F	28. T	29. F	30. F
31. F	32. T	33. T	34. F	

Multiple Choice

1. d	2. c	3. d	4. b	5. b
6. c	7. d	8. c	9. d	10. a

Chapter 17

True-False

1. T	2. F	3. F	4. F	5. T
6. T	7. F	8. F	9. T	10. T
11. T	12. T	13. T	14. F	15. T
16. F				

Multiple Choice

1. d	2. e	3. c	4. c	5. a
6. e	7. e	8. b	9. d	10. e

APPENDIX A

USING THE CALCULATOR TO COMPUTE TABLE VALUES

Note: See that the memory is cleared; you are in the correct mode for financial calculations; and have adequate decimal places.

Appendix B (Compound sum of $1): $FVIF_{i,n} = \$1(1+i)^n$

Hewlett-Packard HP-12C

| 1 | CHS | PV | No. of periods (Days, mths., or yrs.) | N | Interest rate per period | I | 0 | PMT | FV | → | ANSWER |

Hewlett-Packard HP-17B II, HP-19B II

| 1 | +/- | PV | No. of periods (Days, mths., or yrs.) | N | Interest rate per period | I%YR | 0 | PMT | FV | → | ANSWER |

Texas Instruments BA-35

| 1 | +/- | PV | No. of periods (Days, mths., or yrs.) | N | Interest rate per period | %I | 0 | PMT | CPT | FV | → | ANSWER |

Texas Instruments BAII

| 1 | +/- | PV | No. of periods (Days, mths., or yrs.) | N | Interest rate per period | %I | 0 | PMT | 2nd | FV | → | ANSWER |

Texas Instruments BAII Plus

| 1 | +/- | PV | No. of periods (Days, mths., or yrs.) | N | Interest rate per period | I/Y | 0 | PMT | CPT | FV | → | ANSWER |

Appendix C (Present value of $1): $PVIF_{i,n} = \dfrac{\$1}{(1+i)^n}$

Hewlett-Packard HP-12C

| 1 | CHS | FV | No. of periods (Days, mths., or yrs.) | N | Interest rate per period | I | 0 | PMT | PV | → | ANSWER |

Hewlett-Packard HP-17B II, HP-19B II

| 1 | +/- | FV | No. of periods (Days, mths., or yrs.) | N | Interest rate per period | I%YR | 0 | PMT | PV | → | ANSWER |

Texas Instruments BA-35

| 1 | +/- | FV | No. of periods (Days, mths., or yrs.) | N | Interest rate per period | %I | 0 | PMT | CPT | PV | → | ANSWER |

Texas Instruments BAII

| 1 | +/- | FV | No. of periods (Days, mths., or yrs.) | N | Interest rate per period | %I | 0 | PMT | 2nd | PV | → | ANSWER |

Texas Instruments BAII Plus

| 1 | +/- | FV | No. of periods (Days, mths., or yrs.) | N | Interest rate per period | I/Y | 0 | PMT | CPT | PV | → | ANSWER |

Appendix D (Sum of an annuity of $1): $FVIFA_{i,n} = \$1 \sum_{t=0}^{n-1} (1+i)^t$

Hewlett-Packard HP-12C

1 [CHS] [PMT] (No. of periods (Days, mths., or yrs.)) [N] (Interest rate per period) [i] 0 [PV] [FV] → ANSWER

Hewlett-Packard HP-17B II, HP-19B II

1 [+/-] [PMT] (No. of periods (Days, mths., or yrs.)) [N] (Interest rate per period) [I%YR] 0 [PV] [FV] → ANSWER

Texas Instruments BA-35

1 [+/-] [PMT] (No. of periods (Days, mths., or yrs.)) [N] (Interest rate per period) [%i] 0 [PV] [CPT] [FV] → ANSWER

Texas Instruments BAII

1 [+/-] [PMT] (No. of periods (Days, mths., or yrs.)) [N] (Interest rate per period) [%i] 0 [PV] [2nd] [FV] → ANSWER

Texas Instruments BAII Plus

1 [+/-] [PMT] (No. of periods (Days, mths., or yrs.)) [N] (Interest rate per period) [I/Y] 0 [PV] [CPT] [FV] → ANSWER

Appendix E (Present value of an annuity of $1): $PVIFA_{i,n} = \left(\sum_{t=1}^{n} \frac{\$1}{(1+i)^t} \right)$

Hewlett-Packard HP-12C

1 [CHS] [PMT] (No. of periods (Days, mths., or yrs.)) [N] (Interest rate per period) [i] 0 [FV] [PV] → ANSWER

Hewlett-Packard HP-17B II, HP-19B II

1 [+/-] [PMT] (No. of periods (Days, mths., or yrs.)) [N] (Interest rate per period) [I%YR] 0 [FV] [PV] → ANSWER

Texas Instruments BA-35

1 [+/-] [PMT] (No. of periods (Days, mths., or yrs.)) [N] (Interest rate per period) [%i] 0 [FV] [CPT] [PV] → ANSWER

Texas Instruments BAII

1 [+/-] [PMT] (No. of periods (Days, mths., or yrs.)) [N] (Interest rate per period) [%i] 0 [FV] [2nd] [PV] → ANSWER

Texas Instruments BAII Plus

1 [+/-] [PMT] (No. of periods (Days, mths., or yrs.)) [N] (Interest rate per period) [I/Y] 0 [FV] [CPT] [PV] → ANSWER